PLAYING CARDS
AND THEIR STORY

PLAYING CARDS
AND THEIR STORY

With 91 illustrations in the text and 37 plates
including 8 in colour

GEORGE BEAL

ARCO PUBLISHING COMPANY, INC
New York

Published 1975 by Arco Publishing Company Inc.
219 Park Avenue South New York N.Y. 10003

Library of Congress Catalog Card
Number 74-81797

ISBN 0-668-03628-1

Printed in Great Britain

CONTENTS

1
IN THE BEGINNING

It is remarkable that playing-cards have survived for so long. We do not know exactly how long, nor do we know where they originated. Theories, of course, abound: some assert that, like so many unexplained mysteries, they came from the East, or that they were brought back from the Holy Land by Crusaders, or even that they were spread throughout the world by bands of wandering gypsies.

There is no evidence that these are more than suppositions, and in any case, none gives us any clue as to the *origin* of playing-cards. Such games as ludo, Monopoly and lawn tennis were invented in recent times, and we know precisely who invented them, and when. But playing-cards, like chess and draughts, are of ancient and unknown origin, and we have only a few clues to suggest where they might have come from.

Playing-cards of some sort are known to have existed in China from early times, although none has survived from a period earlier than the eighteenth century. A Chinese encyclopedia published in AD 1678 refers to them, and actually gives the year AD 1120 as the date of their invention, a statement which is open to some doubt. Korean cards also have some claim to antiquity, but no early references exist. Dr Stewart Culin, writing at the end of the last century on this subject, stated his belief that both Chinese and Korean cards were derived from a combination of the Korean divinatory arrow and Chinese paper money.

Earliest references to Indian playing-cards date from the beginning of the sixteenth century, 150 years after they were known in Europe, and well after the establishment of communications by the Portuguese and others between Europe and India. Outside Europe, the Islamic countries bordering the Mediterranean are the only other places from which playing-cards could have originated but, until very recently, there was no evidence at all that they had existed in those countries.

This leaves only Europe, and even here early records mentioning playing-cards are scanty. No mention is made of them in an instruction to clerics issued by a French ecclesiastical authority in 1363, which expressly bans dice and games of chance; nor are they referred to in a similar ban against gaming issued in France in 1369 by Charles V. Petrarch (1304–74), who wrote a treatise on the subject of gaming, does not once mention playing-cards, and neither do Giovanni Boccaccio (1313–75) and Geoffrey Chaucer (1340–1400), both of whom made reference to other forms of gaming in their works.

The earliest European reference to the subject occurs in a Latin manuscript written by a German monk named Johannes, and preserved in the British Museum. Translated, the manuscript reads:

Hence it is that a certain game called the game of cards has come to us in this year, viz., the year of our Lord MCCCLXXVII [1377]. In which game the state of the world as it now is is excellently described and figured. But at what time it was invented, where, and by whom I am entirely ignorant. But the subject of this treatise may be compared with the game of chess, for in both these are kings, queens and chief nobles, and common people, so that both games may be treated in a moral sense.

In the game which men call the game of cards they paint the cards in different manners, and they play with them in one way and another. For the common form and as it came to us is thus, viz., four kings are depicted on four cards, each of whom sits on a royal throne. And each holds a certain sign in his hand, of which signs some are reputed good, but others signify evil. Under which kings are two *marschalli*, the first of whom holds the sign upwards in his hand, in the same manner as the king; but the other holds the same sign downwards in his hand.

After this there are other ten cards, outwardly of the same size and shape, on the first of which the aforesaid king's sign is placed once; on the second twice; and so on with the others up to the tenth card inclusive. And so each king becomes the thirteenth, and there will be altogether fifty-two cards.

Of this manuscript's authenticity there seems little doubt, even though it is a copy dated 1472. Less than a hundred years had elapsed since the original had been written, which makes the likelihood of interpolation fairly remote.

This, then, clearly establishes the existence of playing-cards in the third quarter of the fourteenth century, and we can safely assume that they came into use somewhat earlier. Feliciano Bussi, in his *History of the City of Viterbo* (1743), quotes an earlier chronicler, Giovanni de Covelluzzo, writing in the fifteenth century: 'In the year 1379, was brought into Viterbo the game of cards, which comes from Seracinia [country of the Saracens?] and is with them called *Naib*.' This, if authentic, is the first known reference which connects playing-cards with an Islamic country. A later reference to the same subject appears in Malespini's *History of Florence* (1728), which refers to the *Chronicles* of Giovanni Morelli dated 1393. This also mentions *Naibi* as a kind of game.

The Spanish word for 'playing-cards' even today is *naipes*, and the Spaniards had been influenced by an Islamic people – the Moors. The implication is clear enough: the Spanish word for playing-cards was derived from an Islamic source. *Naib*, or more correctly, *na'ib*, is an Arabic word meaning 'deputy', which, on first examination, seems an unlikely name for a pack of cards.

Dr Stewart Culin states categorically that playing-cards existed in China in or before the twelfth century, and were introduced from there to Europe during the fifteenth century. William Andrew Chatto, on the other hand, writing in 1848, suggested that the true place of origin of playing-cards was India.

There was, and still is, a tendency to ascribe all sorts of unexplained inventions to the East without a great deal of evidence. After all, the Chinese were making block prints long before we had invented printing in Europe, and the Indians probably invented chess, so why should playing-cards not have originated in the East too?

There is no evidence that the earliest European cards had any connection with China or India, and in any case, both Chinese and Indian cards are quite unlike normal European cards in appearance. Chatto, with some logic, connects the game of chess with playing-cards, for there are some parallels. Among versions of chess known in the East is a four-sided game, whose pieces include four kings, elephants, horses and chariots, together with a number of foot-soldiers or pawns. Even the earliest European packs known had four kings, while the rest of the pieces from a four-sided game of chess could have formed the basis of the other court cards.

Chess, it appears, passed from India to Persia, an Islamic country, and from there the game travelled to the Arabs, who passed it on to Europe sometime before, or during, the eleventh century. Is it possible that the Arabs themselves developed a card game from chess, and if they did, was that also passed on to Europe?

It has, at various times, been suggested that playing-cards have been brought to Europe either by returning Crusaders, or by roving bands of gypsies. The last true Crusade ended in 1291, and playing-cards, so far as can be deduced, were unknown until almost one hundred years later.

The theory that the gypsies brought playing-cards to Europe is advanced by, among others, the Reverend E. S. Taylor in his book *The History of Playing Cards* (1865). Taylor's ideas are largely speculation, and the 'gypsy theory' has since been dismissed on the grounds that the first Romanies appeared in Europe in 1398, by which time, of course, playing-cards were well known. It is questionable, however, whether this date can be substantiated.

The gypsies did pass through the Turkish Empire, so there remains at least the possibility that they could have acquired playing-cards there had they existed. The Islamic religion frowns upon gambling in all its forms, and the graphic portrayal of human or animal forms, while not actually contrary to Islamic law, is rarely done. On the other hand, we know that playing-cards have existed and do exist in Persia and the Islamic communities of India.

In 1939, however, Professor L. A. Mayer wrote an article in a Cairo journal dealing with a pack of

PLATE 1
The numerical card 'seven' as seen in three suitmark systems: A. French and international; B. German and Central European; C. Swiss.

8

Vereinigte
Altenburger und Stralsunder
Spielkarten-Fabriken A.-G.
Leinfelden b. Stuttgart

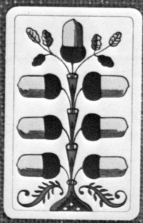
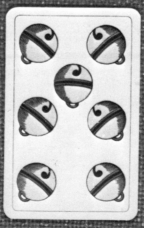

cards discovered in the Topkapi Sarayi Museum in Istanbul. At the time, the article made little impact, but it was reprinted, together with photographs of the pack, in 1971, when the professor's work received much closer attention.

Professor Mayer describes a pack of *Mamluk* (or Mameluke) cards, which are unquestionably the first genuine example of playing-cards originating in a Mediterranean Islamic country. The Mamelukes were a class of former slaves from Turkey, who took power in Egypt in 1254, ruling that country until 1517.

The Mameluke pack is dated by Professor Mayer as being fifteenth century, but another card fragment found in Egypt since his article was written in 1939 is even older, possibly as early as twelfth century. Naturally, the presence of such cards at an early date offers reasonable evidence for assuming that playing-cards in fact originated outside Europe.

The cards in the Mameluke pack are about 252mm × 95mm in size, and bear designs which are immediately recognisable as close relatives of the early Italian patterns. Mayer believed the pack to contain 5 suits: Cups, Coins, Swords, Polo-sticks and Staffs, but it now seems likely that the last two suits are in fact one.

The Arabic inscriptions on the court-cards supply confirmatory evidence for the origin of the word *na'ib* as applied to a pack of cards, for they are shown as: *Malik* (king); *Na'ib Malik* (deputy king, governor or viceroy); and *Na'ib Thani* (deputy governor). Although it is incomplete, it is possible to reconstruct the Mameluke pack, which would take this form:

Four suits: Cups, Coins, Swords and Polo-sticks (or Staffs).

Each suit: Three court-cards: King, Viceroy and Deputy; 10 numerical cards, 1–10.

Being long and narrow, the Mameluke cards are differently shaped from the earliest-known European packs. On the other hand, the original card from which the fragment found in Egypt was taken would have been 116mm × 78mm, producing a card very close to the Italian format which has

1. Islamic (Mameluke) cards from fifteenth-century Egypt: (*left*) Malik of Cups; and (*right*) Seven of Swords

always been somewhat narrower than other European patterns.

It has been argued that the Islamic cards could have been derived from European originals, rather than the other way around, but the fact that the word *na'ib* has found its way into two European languages to mean 'playing-cards' seems enough to confirm the belief that our modern packs of cards are descendants of an Arabic original introduced into Europe sometime after the thirteenth century.

The position today is that 3 basic suit-systems exist in European and European-derived packs. All use 4 suits, which are:

Italy and Spain: Cups, Swords, Money (or Coins) and Batons

Germany and Central Europe: Hearts, Bells, Leaves and Acorns; with a variation for Switzerland, which has Shields and Flowers instead of Hearts and Leaves

France, Britain, USA and international: Hearts, Clubs, Diamonds and Spades.

2
PLAYING-CARDS WITH ITALIAN SUITS

Indications are that the first playing-cards known in Europe were Italian. Johannes the monk does not give us any details of the appearance of the cards he mentions, but the evidence of Covelluzzo gives us the date of 1379 for the pack of 'Saracenic' cards seen in Viterbo.

Packs of cards with suits of Cups, Coins, Swords and Batons were certainly known very early in Italy, and these later developed into a number of definite regional patterns of the states into which the country was then divided. Similar suitmarks were also adopted in Spain and Portugal.

Italian suits proper are found on cards in the northern part of the country, while further south, packs are used employing the less complicated Spanish-type suitmarks. Because there are differences between Spanish packs and those used in southern Italy, suitmarks on packs from the latter area are known as Italo-Spanish type (Addenda, p 112).

Italian suitmarks have become so stylised that it is sometimes not easy to recognise the emblems such as Cups, which are a formalised version of a type of ecclesiastical chalice. Moreover, a very typical characteristic of Italian suits is the way the sheaves of swords and batons are interwoven on the numerical cards of those suits.

Italian names of the suits are: *Coppe* (Cups); *Danari* or *Denari* (Coins); *Spade* (Swords) and *Bastoni* (Batons). Probably the most typical of the Italian-suited packs are those found in the Venetian area, which include several localised versions of similar design.

Venetian pattern (*Venete, Trevigiane or Trevisane telate*)
The cards are so named from Venice itself or from Treviso, another town in the area. A Venetian-pattern pack usually contains 40 cards, although the

2. Venetian pattern: King of Batons and Ace of Cups

occasional 52-card pack is known. Each suit contains 3 court-cards: King, Knight and Jack (*Re, Cavallo* and *Fante*), and numerical cards 7–2 (or 10–2 in the case of 52-card packs), together with the Ace. Cards are, like most north Italian packs, long and narrow, measuring about 102mm × 50mm. Modern court-cards arc double-ended, a characteristic since the early nineteenth century.

A distinguishing feature of the Venetian pack is the presence of mottoes on the Aces, which read: on Cups, *Per un punto Martin perse la capa* (For a point Martin lost his cloak); on Money, *Non val saper a chi ha fortuna contra* (It's not worth knowing someone whose luck is always out) – this is sometimes completely omitted; on Swords, *Non ti fidar de me se il cuor ti manca* (Don't put your trust in me if you have no heart to); and on Batons, *Se ti perdi tuo dano* (If you lose, you're damned).

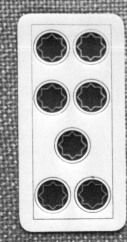

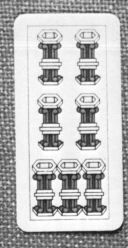

A

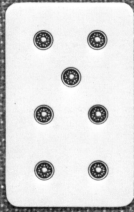
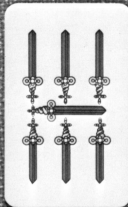

B

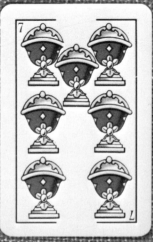

C

At the centre of the King of Batons card is a shield bearing the arms of the town of Treviso, and the word *Tarvisium*, the Latin name for the place. All Knights are mounted, while the Knight of Swords flourishes his sword above his head, with the Jack of that suit holding his sword point downwards. An extra head, apparently transfixed upon the end of the sword appearing from the other half of the card appears at the centre. The figure of Mercury appears on the Two of Swords, a lady carrying a garland on the Four, and another woman carrying a basket and a branch on the Six. The Italian tax stamp usually appears on the Ace of Coins, and the maker's name on the Four.

Trentine pattern (*Trentine Italiane telate*)

Italian-suited packs from the north of Italy have a family resemblance which suggests a common origin for the design, and the Trentine pattern is no exception. Named after the town of Trento, the pattern is found in packs of 52 or 40 cards, which measure about 100mm × 55mm. For 40-card packs, the Ten, Nine and Eight of each suit is suppressed. Usually single-ended, the Trentine pattern's closest relatives are the *Bresciane* and *Bergamasche* patterns.

The Trentine pattern also resembles the Venetian, but omits mottoes on the Aces. Particular points of recognition are: the Italian tax stamp appears on the King of Coins, while the Ace appears to have no suitmark except an oval at the centre bearing the portrait of a young man; indices on the numerical cards are shown, and numbers are also superimposed upon the suitmarks themselves. These numbers appear at the top of the Cups and at the intersections of the crossed Swords and Batons. A small vignetted picture appears on the Four of Coins, often a sailing ship.

Bresciane pattern (*Bresciane telate*)

This pack is so named after the town of Brescia, and is a very close relative of the Trentine pattern. The 40 cards are usually smaller, however, measuring about 90mm × 43mm, and are single-ended. The figures on the court-cards are clean-shaven, and there are no mottoes on the Aces. The maker's name

PLATE 2
The numerical card 'seven' as seen in three suitmark systems: A. Italian; B. Italo-Spanish; C. Spanish.

3. Trentine pattern: King of Money and Ace of Money

4. Bresciane pattern: King of Batons and Knight of Money

usually appears on the King of Batons and the Knight of Coins, and there appears to be no card to carry the tax stamp.

The Knight of Coins has a somewhat strange appearance, since the head of his horse has been turned backwards rather awkwardly, so that the animal is looking along the rear half of the body. Instead of a garland, the woman on the Four of Swords is carrying a large branch, while the Italian coat of arms appears on the Two of Swords. As also

13

5. Bergamasche pattern: King of Swords and Knight of Cups

6. Triestine pattern: King of Money and Jack of Batons

with the Trentine, the Cupid remains perched upon the top of the Cup on the Ace card.

Bergamasche pattern (Bergamasche telate)
This is another localised version of the Trentine pattern, being named after the town of Bergamo. Bergamasche packs contain 40 cards, and are double-ended, measuring about 93mm × 50mm. Court figures are again clean-shaven. The word VINCERAI appears on the Ace of Batons, crossed bugles on the Two of Swords, and a pair of scales on the Four of Coins. The figure of Cupid appears on

the Ace of Cups, as with the Trentine and Bresciane patterns, but the little dog which appears with the Jack of Cups in both the last-named has disappeared in the Bergamasche. There are no mottoes on the Aces.

Triestine pattern (Triestine telate)
The fact that this pack has mottoes on the Aces, together with a general overall resemblance, indicates a connection with the Venetian pattern and its relatives. Named after the city of Trieste, the packs contain either 52 or 40 cards, measuring about 96mm × 53mm. The cards are double-ended and indexed, while a special feature is that the name of each court-card is placed on a panel at the centre of each card.

Thus, the King of Coins (indexed with the number 13) is inscribed *Re di Danari* the Knight of Cups (indexed with the number 12) is inscribed *Caval di Coppe*, and the Jack of Swords (indexed as number 11) is shown as *Fante di Spade*.

The mottoes on the Aces vary from those of the Venetian pattern, reading: on the Ace of Cups, *Una coppa de buon vin fa coraggio mor bin* (A goblet of good wine gives you the courage to die well); on Coins, *Non val saper chi ha fortuna contra* (as with the Venetian pattern); on Swords *Il giuoco della spada a molti non aggrada* (Swordplay is not to everybody's liking); and on Batons, *Molte volte le giucocate van finire a bastonate* (Games will often end in blows). These spellings, of course, do not accord with literary Italian, probably due to the use of dialect words or to the revision or rationalisation of Italian spelling since the mottoes first appeared.

The Italian tax stamp, as with the Venetian and Bergamasche, appears on the Ace of Coins, while the maker's name usually appears on the Ace of Coins and on the Two of Swords. Fifty-two-card packs consist of King, Knight, Jack, 10–2 and Ace in

PLATE 3
Variations on the English pattern: A. A smiling Queen of Hearts from a De La Rue pack of c1880; B. From the USA, a 'four-colour' pack, each suitmark in a different colour; C. An extra suit of Rackets, also from the USA; D. A black-background pack; E. A French version by Camoin; F. A Spanish version (the King has two left hands!); G. A barrel-shaped pack from Japan; H. A modern version from Sweden; J. 'Mikimoto' from Japan.

A

B

C

D

E

F

G

H

J

7. Bolognese pattern: King of Cups and Ace of Swords

8. Trappola cards: King of Coins and Knight of Batons

each suit, but for 40-card packs, the Ten, Nine and Eight are suppressed.

Bolognese pattern (*Bolognese telate*)
To all intents and purposes, this is the Bolognese Tarot pack (qv) minus the Queens and 22 trump

cards. However, there are some differences, and the cards are regularly sold as a separate pack.

Named after the city of Bologna, the cards are usually 40 to a pack, measuring about 100mm × 50mm. Court-cards are King, Knight and Jack, with numerical cards from 7–2, plus Aces. The cards have no ruled border around the edge.

The design is quite distinctive from other Italian-suited packs, and one peculiarity is that the Aces have been given such debased suitmarks that they are almost unrecognisable. Very close examination of the Ace of Cups does make it possible to discern a 'cup', which is surmounted by a crown; the Ace of Coins carries the tax stamp and very little else; the Ace of Swords has a crown from which issues a long-necked bird's head (actually the curved blade of a sword which ends as a bird's head); and the Ace of Batons carries the end of a Baton from the centre of a crown.

Except for the King of Coins, who carries his suitmark in his hand, with one on each side of his head, the Kings of the pack are shown beardless. The King of Cups is, in fact, the Queen of Cups from the Tarot pack, shows two suitmarks, but has a strangely-deformed right hand which seems to have somehow become joined to the suitmark. Further details of the Tarot pack are given under the section dealing with Tarots.

COLOUR PLATE I
A. A Cavalier of Cups from a German Trappola pack dated c1895. Made by Ludwig & Schmidt.
B. A Cavalier of Clubs from a French Tarot pack, made c1900 by B. P. Grimaud.
C. Trump No 17 from a German animal Tarot pack by Fr Aug Dreissig of Tondorf bei Erfurt, c1800.
D. The Shah, a court-card from a Persian pack, probably made during the mid-nineteenth century.
E. A Jack of Money from a pack made in Bologna, Italy, c1840.
F. A geographical pack made in Italy c1670. The card is the Jack of Spades.
G. Trump No 35 – the Twins – from a Minchiate pack made in Italy c1790.
H. Another Minchiate card from a pack made in Italy c1800. This card depicts the Fool.
J. Made in East Germany, this modern reprint is of the Jost Ammon pack, originally issued in 1588. Here is the Three of Drinking Cups.

A

B

C

D

E

F

G

H

J

A

B

C

D

E

F

G

H

J

Trappola cards

Trappola is a card game, apparently of Italian origin, but it seems to have taken root in Austria-Hungary where the cards were once well known. As a game, it appears to have died out, and the cards are therefore no longer produced. In Greece ordinary French-suited cards are referred to as *Ellenike Trapoula* or Greek cards. This somewhat misleading use of the word 'trappola' has been applied elsewhere in Europe, usually to describe any pack of unusual appearance.

True trappola cards use Italian suits, and packs contain 36 cards, consisting of King, Knight, Jack, numerical cards 10–7, Deuce and Ace. Both double- and single-ended packs have been produced, and sizes of cards vary, with some packs as small as 100mm × 45mm or as large as 140mm × 60mm.

Trappola cards were used in Austria, Bohemia (now part of Czechoslovakia) and Silesia, which now forms part of Poland. The game was certainly known until World War II, and in fact, was known in Poland under the name *Traplaczka*.

The numerical cards of each suit were numbered in Roman figures X–VII, and II and I for the Deuce and Ace. The tax stamp (probably with a German inscription) usually appears on the Ace of Swords, or sometimes the Ten of Coins, with the maker's name on the Ace of Batons, the Deuce of Swords or the Ace of Coins. Verses are sometimes incorporated in the design.

Makers of trappola cards included Ferdinand Piatnik of Vienna, Johann Georg Pichler of Linz, Peter Schachner of Wels, Josef Gezek of Prague, Friedrich Eurich of Linz, J. C. DuPort of Warsaw, ASS, and Ludwig & Schmidt of Halle.

Designs of trappola cards generally have a somewhat primitive appearance, with the courts of the Coins and Batons suits wearing seventeenth-century type of costume. The Kings, who appear to be sitting on low brick walls, wear hats which incorporate crowns. The Coins suit sometimes uses suitmarks which resemble flowers.

Generally speaking, trappola cards seem to have some connection with an earlier – now lost – Tarot pack, but minus the trump cards, Queens and numerical cards III to VI,

3

ITALO-SPANISH SUITMARKS

Certain regional cards in Italy form a special group in that they use suitmarks more akin to those used in Spain, and they have therefore been termed Italo-Spanish-suited cards. They are usually smaller and more square than the Italian-suited cards of the north, while the suitmarks are much easier to recognise. The cards are, however, quite different in appearance from the packs used in Spain, and have a number of characteristics which distinguish them from both Spanish-suited and Italian-suited packs. There are four regional packs using such suitmarks:

Neapolitan pattern (*Napoletane*, or *Baresi telate*)
Naples and Bari were two duchies which became part of the Kingdom of the Two Sicilies, and this pattern of cards (together with the Sicilian) developed within the borders of that kingdom. The Neapolitan or Bari pack contains 40 small cards measuring about 83mm × 52mm. The figures on the court-cards (King, Knight and Jack) are single-ended, and use a unique method to confirm the suits to which they belong. All court figures stand on coloured bases, the colours being arranged to coincide with the suits: yellow for Coins, red for Cups, green for Batons and blue for Swords. Thus, the King of Coins stands on a yellow base, and the Knight of Batons stands on a green one.

The Ace of Coins, which carries the tax stamp, shows a two-headed eagle, and usually the name of the maker. Furled Italian flags behind a shield appear on the Four of Coins, a mask-like face on the Three of Batons, vignetted, silhouetted figures on the Five of Swords (a hunting scene, or an artist at work) which are usually repeated at each end, while the Jack of Swords holds a green branch in his right hand, and his sword pointing downwards in his left. As with all cards in this group, the designs appear on plain white grounds, with no ruled border.

Sicilian pattern (*Siciliane telate*)
Sicily, of course, was the other part of the kingdom which included Naples and Bari, and it is not surprising, therefore, to find that the Sicilian pack closely resembles the Neapolitan. Of similar size (about 80mm × 50mm), the court-cards are single-ended as well. There are 40 cards to the pack (King, Knight, Jack, numerical cards 7–2 and Ace), with coloured bases for the figures. With the Sicilian pattern, the coloured bases are used differently, the colour denoting the status of the card. A green base indicates a King, a yellow base a Knight, and a Jack stands on a red ground.

The Ace of Coins carries the tax stamp, which is superimposed on a single-headed eagle. This card normally shows the name of the maker. Other dis-

9. Neapolitan pattern: King of Cups and Jack of Swords

PLATE 4
A. 'Baroque' by Piatnik, 1961 version; B. The same, but an earlier design; C. 'Luxury' by Piatnik; D. 'Salon-Karte 66' by VEB Altenburg; E. 'Portrait' by VEB Altenburg; F. Dutch non-standard by Speelkaarten Nederland; G. 'Baroness' by ASS; H. 'Jeu Louis XV' by Grimaud; J. 'Chambord' by Héron.

A

B

C

D

E

F

G

H

J

10. Sicilian pattern: King of Batons and Knight of Swords

11. Piacentine pattern: Knight of Money and Ace of Money

tinguishing marks are: a pedlar holding a fan on the Three of Coins, a sailing ship on the Six of Cups, a fish on the Two, a house on the Three, and fencers on the Four.

The design of the suitmark on the Coins suit commonly shows a device of three legs joined at the centre, like the Isle of Man symbol. The Batons suit has a drinking-glass on the Seven, and a similar image appears on the Three of Swords. Also on the Swords suit are: on the Seven, a pitcher, on the Six, a ship, on the Five, a dog holding a package in its mouth, on the Four and Two, a dog again, and on the Ace, a house.

Piacentine pattern (Piacentine telate)

This pack takes its name from the city of Piacenza, capital of the province of the same name, although the cards are used throughout the provinces along the western side of Italy. The cards are more like the usual narrow Italian types, measuring about 92mm × 50mm. There are 40 cards to a pack, each suit containing King, Knight, Jack, numerical cards from 7–2, and Ace. Packs are found with both single- and double-ended courts.

The Ace of Coins, with its crowned, single-headed eagle, shows the tax stamp and also the name of the maker. The design of the Coins suit usually shows a face at the centre of each suitmark. The King of Coins is shown holding an axe in his left hand, the Knight of that suit holds a small shield, and the Four has a wreath surrounding a coat of arms. The Knight, whose horse faces away from the front, appears either to be riding backwards or side-saddle. The King of Cups holds the suitmark in his left hand and a spear in his right; the Jack holds a spear in his right hand, and has a sheathed sword at his left; the Knight of Batons faces away from the front, and the Jack of that suit has a Baton bearing a crown. The Ace of Swords shows a Cupid grasping a giant sword, and surrounded by a garland. Usually, all figures of the courts are clean-shaven except

PLATE 5

A. A Swedish pattern pack, as made by Piatnik; B, C and D. Some variations on the Swedish pattern; E. 'Vaakuna', a Swedish pattern pack as used in Finland; F. 'Turun Linna', a barrel-shaped non-standard pack from Finland; G. 'Standard No 97' by Piatnik; H. Danish 'standard' pack by Holmblad; J. 'Regentkort' by Öberg, Sweden.

A

B

C

D

E

F

G

H

J

for the moustached Knight of Cups and Jack of Swords.

Romagnole pattern (*Romagnole telate*)

This pack is named after the district of Romagna, which was one of the old States of the Church, although the cards were used in a wider area than that.

The cards, which are single-ended, measure about 90mm × 50mm, and are 40 to the pack, each suit consisting of King, Knight, Jack, numerical cards 7–2, and Ace. The court-card figures, except the Kings, stand on bases like those of Sicilian and Neapolitan cards, but the colours appear to have no significance. The pack bears some resemblance to the Piacentine pattern, with its King of Coins holding an axe, King of Cups with a mace, and Jack of Cups with a spear. The Cupid also appears on the Ace of Swords.

All the Kings are bearded, all the Knights moustached, and all the Jacks clean-shaven. The Jacks of Coins and Cups wear pantaloons.

12. Romagnole pattern: King of Swords and Jack of Cups

4
CARDS WITH SPANISH SUITMARKS

Playing-cards were probably first known in the Iberian peninsula during the late fifteenth century, although a writer, the Abbé de la Rive, has claimed that they were actually invented in Spain. De la Rive's sources are questionable to say the least. However, playing-cards were commonly used by Spaniards from the sixteenth century onwards, since the Spanish historian Antonio de Herrera tells how the Aztecs of Mexico were interested to see Spaniards playing cards in 1519.

Both Spanish and Portuguese used similar cards, and, during the years of exploration and discovery, carried playing-cards to the Americas, the Indies, both East and West, and to Japan.

Spanish suitmarks, like those of Italy, are Cups (*Copas*), Coins (*Oros*), Swords (*Espadas*) and Batons (*Bastos*), but they differ from the Italian type by the simplicity and realism of their design. Packs using Spanish-suited cards are found not only in Spain, but in France, Sardinia, Latin America, and of course in Spanish colonies and overseas territories. Portugal has since given up the use of the suitmarks, and now uses French-suited cards.

According to the sixteenth-century writer Garcilaso de la Vega the Spanish were so fond of cards that on finding themselves without proper packs in the New World they made their own packs from leaves and leather. Until quite recently, it was still possible to find crude playing-cards made from deerskin and other materials, marked with recognisable Spanish suitmarks, in use by the Indians of the south-western areas of the United States.

Standard Spanish pattern
Today, Spanish packs contain either 40 or 48 cards. There are 3 court-cards: King, Knight and Jack. Kings are always shown standing erect, never seated, as in Italian packs. The Knight is mounted,

13. Standard Spanish pattern: King of Batons and Jack of Money

while the Knave stands. Packs are found both single- and double-ended, and are indexed in the Spanish fashion with numbers only. Kings are numbered 12, Knights are indexed 11, and Jacks as 10, while the numerical cards bear similar numbers down to the Ace, which is numbered 1. In 40-card packs, Eights and Nines are omitted.

It has also become customary (since the beginning of the nineteenth century) for Spanish cards to indicate the suit by a code-system of line-breaks in the ruled border at the top and bottom of each card. Thus, the Coins suit has no breaks or gaps, but Cups have one break, Swords have two, and Batons have three.

Spanish courts now are typically unstylised having a somewhat straight 'illustration' look, unlike Italian-suited cards. The Five of Swords usually bears the tax stamp, and the Ace of Coins is normally quite decorative, showing a large coin surrounded by flags, and the maker's name and address. The

14. Catalan pattern: King of Swords and Jack of Money

15. Sarde pattern: King of Money and Jack of Cups

Four of Cups is often used for giving details of the maker, together with various decorative devices. Cards average 100mm × 60mm in size.

Catalan pattern (Cartes Catalanes)
This is a Spanish-type pack found in south-western France. It follows the usual Spanish rule in having indices from 12 to 1, there being 48 cards to a pack. The cards are single-ended, about 96mm × 63mm in size. As with regular Spanish packs, the border-breaks indicating the suits are shown in the top and bottom margins.

Kings are standing, but have their legs hidden by their robes, the King of Cups carrying a long sceptre in his left hand. The other court-card figures appear to be standing either on grass or on the edge of a

parkland, with the Jack of Coins holding a hunting-horn in his left hand. In Spanish packs proper, the Clubs or Batons are usually coloured green, but in the Catalan pack, colours of the court-card suit-marks of this suit are usually King – green; Knight – blue; and Jack – red. The maker's name usually appears on the Ace of Coins.

Sarde or Sardinian pattern (Carte Sarde)
Since it comes from the island of Sardinia, this pack could be regarded as an Italian regional pattern; but unlike other Italian packs, it follows the Spanish style quite closely. Based on an old Spanish pattern dating from 1810, the Sardinian pattern is found in packs containing 40 cards: King, Knight, Jack, numerical cards from 7–2 and the Ace. Cards, which are about 87mm × 57mm in size, have the appearance of a coloured engraving, and unlike regular Spanish cards, have no border breaks, although the corners carry the usual Spanish indices from 12 to 1.

The court figures stand in the foreground of various scenes, those of the Swords suit depicting men on a battlefield. The costumes appear to be sixteenth-century, with the Swords courts wearing armour. The Cups suitmark is rather more elaborate than usual, the Ace showing a large vase-like Cup festooned with vines and bunches of grapes. The other Aces and Fours are all very decorative: on the Four of Swords is a scene showing a warrior giving the *coup de grâce* to a fallen enemy, and on the Ace is a Cupid holding a large sword surrounded by flags, cannon-balls, a cannon and tents. The Four of Batons shows a robed figure sitting on a seat before a castle, while the Ace shows a Cupid holding the Baton. The Four of Cups shows a reclining figure of a female attended by a Cupid, and the Four of Coins shows a soldier and a woman sitting side by side. The Ace of Coins carries the tax stamp.

Aluette pattern (Cartes d'Aluette)
Aluette is a French card game which uses Spanish-

PLATE 6
A. A Dondorf pack, c1935; B. Piatnik pack, c1930; C. Hungarian pack, originally a Piatnik design called 'Whistspiel No 187'; D. 'Königin' by ASS, originally a Dondorf design; E. 'Comtesse' by Bielefeld; F. 'Richelieu' by Müller; G. 'Marguerite' by Müller; H. 'Club Bridge' by Modiano; J. 'Poker Luxe' by Masenghini.

A

B

C

D

E

F

G

H

J

16. Aluette pattern: King of Money and Knight of Batons

suited cards, and is still played in Brittany and along the west coast of France, where it is popular among the sea-faring community. The design of the present pack can be traced to a card-maker named Pierre Sigogne of Nantes (1776–81). The similarity of his name to *cigogne* (stork) led him to use the stork as a trade-mark, and the wrappers for his packs carried a device showing a stork being crowned by an angel. The modern *Aluette* pack continues to follow this theme: on the Three of Cups is a stork placing a wreath upon the head of a woman, and on the Ace of Batons, a stork is placing a cap upon the head of a Cupid.

There are 48 cards to the pack, each about 87mm × 57mm. There are 3 court-cards to a suit: King, Knight (but strangely, a female), and Jack, together with numerical cards 9–2 and Ace. Aluette cards do not follow the Spanish custom of using breaks in the border to signify suits. They are single-ended, and without indices.

There are a number of other peculiarities to the design: the only bearded King is that of the Coins suit, who holds a small axe in his right hand, while the only bearded Jack is that of the Cups suit, who holds a halberd in his right hand. A naked boy surmounted by a wreath appears on a swing between the two suitmarks of the Two of Batons, while a dog looks on; and a North American Indian appears on the Ace of that suit. The Five of Coins shows a man and a woman kissing; the Four shows two interlaced coloured triangles; the Two of Cups has its suitmarks transformed into heads, with storks' bodies appearing on either side of each, while below is a seated cow.

Aluette cards have special names: the *Aluettes* proper being the Three of Coins (or *Monsieur*); the Three of Cups (*Madame*); the Two of Coins (*Le Borgne*, or one-eyed man); and the Two of Cups (*La Vache*, or cow). Then come *Les Doubles*: Nine of Cups and Nine of Coins (*Grand Neuf* and *Petit Neuf*); Two of Batons and Two of Swords (*Deux de Chène* and *Deux d'Ecrit*). The Five of Swords is called *Jarretières de la Mariée* (bride's garters), the Five of Coins is known as *Bise Dure* (strong north wind), the Four of Cups is *Chasse Luette* (roughly, 'tonsil-chaser').

The game is rather a strange one, and depends largely on one's ability to cheat, and on making various signs, such as winking, holding up various fingers, putting out the tongue, and passing the hand through the hair, in order to inform one's partner of certain cards.

5
GERMAN-SUITED PLAYING-CARDS AND SWISS CARDS

By the latter half of the fourteenth century, playing-cards were certainly popular in Germany, since we have the evidence of a prohibition against them in the city of Regensburg (Ratisbon) in Bavaria, dated 1378. German playing-cards were being produced in enormous quantities by 1440, largely for export to various other countries of Europe. Germany was responsible for the introduction of wood-engraving to the Continent, its use having revolutionised the art of card-making. According to the records of the city of Ulm, dated 1474, 'playing-cards were sent in small casks into Italy, Sicily and also over the sea, and bartered for spices and other wares.'

Between the years 1380 and 1384, playing-cards are referred to in the archives of the city of Nuremberg, and only a few years later, mention is made of them in the city records of other German towns such as Augsburg and Stuttgart. A Dominican monk named Ingold says in his book *Das Guldin Spil* (1472) that cards were brought into Germany early in the fourteenth century, most likely by soldiers returning from Italy under Emperor Henry VII (d1313).

Although the first cards to be seen in Germany must have been those from Italy, which naturally bore Italian suitmarks, the German makers were not slow in developing their own particular suitmarks. Surviving today from very early times are what can be' regarded as the German national suitmarks: Hearts (*Herzen*); Hawk-bells (*Schellen*); Leaves (*Grün* or *Laub*); and Acorns (*Eicheln*).

Earlier German packs consisted of 48 cards, each suit containing 3 court-cards and 9 numerical cards. The court-cards were King (*König*); Over-knave (*Obermann*, usually called simply *Ober*); and Under-knave (*Untermann*, or *Unter*). There being no Ace, the highest-value card was the Deuce (*Daus*), and German-suited packs retain these features to this day, although they now omit Threes, Fours and Fives. Originally, Hearts and Bells were coloured red, while Leaves and Acorns were green; but nowadays, only Hearts and Leaves are single-coloured, Acorns and Bells being green, red and yellow.

The early establishment of a national set of suitmarks did not prevent German makers from experimenting with other symbols. Animals were very popular, some packs having suits of Lions, Peacocks, Monkeys and Parrots; while others introduced Hares, Books, Drinking-cups, Printers' Inking Pads, Fishes and even Frying-pans. Many of these packs were beautifully produced and printed from engraved copper plates. Admirable though they were as works of art, they were hardly practicable for card-playing, since it was difficult to remember the signs in the pack. In time, the national suits became generally adopted, not only in Germany proper, but in other Central European countries, like Austria, Bohemia, Poland and Switzerland. The Swiss, however, made changes in two suits.

Although the use of German suits was widespread in Central Europe, the composition and design of packs varied from country to country, and even, in the case of Germany itself, from region to region. Some of these regional packs closely resemble one or two of their neighbours, but it is possible to differentiate ten different designs, of which eight still survive. One was lost during the last century, while the other survived until World War II. (See Addenda p 112.)

German-suited regional packs are:

Linz pattern (*Linzer Bild*)

This pack was known to be in use in Austria during the early half of the nineteenth century. There were either 36 or 32 cards, about 100mm × 55mm in size, to each pack. The cards are single-ended,

A

B

C

D

E

F

G

H

J

usually wood-engraved, and coloured. Thirty-six-card packs consist of King, Ober, Unter, Deuce and numerical cards 10–6 in each suit, while 32-card packs omit the Sixes.

The designs are attractive, if somewhat primitive, most cards being decorated with small vignetted pictures of people and animals. A good distinguishing feature is the man pushing a wheel on the Deuce of Hearts, which has led to the pack being dubbed the 'Wheelpusher' pack. On the Deuce of Bells are two men, one seated at a table, while the other wields a stick. The Deuce of Leaves shows a drunk.

Numerical cards show various flowers: tulips on the Six of Hearts, pinks on the Six of Leaves, Nine of Bells and Eight of Leaves, and an owl on the Six of Bells a camel on the Ten of Acorns a lion on the Ten of Leaves and a hen on the Eight of Bells. The Eight of Acorns shows a flute-player, the Ten of Bells a Chinese, the Nine of Hearts a wood-cutter, the Seven of Acorns shows a rider on a hobby-horse, while the Eight of Hearts shows a tennis-player; a snake is shown on the Seven of Hearts. The costumes throughout are vaguely eighteenth-century. These vignetted designs are probably variable.

Ansbach or *Nuremberg pattern* (*Ansbacher* or *Nürn-bergisches Bild;* occasionally, *Münchener Bild*)
This pack, once used in the Nuremberg area of Germany, is no longer being produced, although examples may still be found in use by local people. Size of cards is about 90mm × 55mm, although smaller, patience-size packs also occur. Packs contain 36 cards, with each suit consisting of King, Ober, Unter, numerical cards 10–6 and Deuce, the court-cards being single-ended. The design is simple, and lacks decoration, while distinctive designs on the Deuces are: on the Deuce of Acorns, the Nuremberg lion with a semi-human face and on the Deuce of Leaves, a scribe looking up at the arms, while apparently writing a date: 18 October

17. Linz pattern: Deuces of Hearts and Bells

18. Ansbach pattern: Unter of Leaves and Deuce of Acorns

1813, the exact significance of which is not clear. The Kings stand in front of their thrones; figures on court-cards (except those of Bells) are shown holding the suitmark. The Unter of Leaves is distinguished by the fact that he holds a stem of the leaf which curves downwards towards the suitmark in an S-shape.

Prussian-Silesian pattern (*Preussisch-Schlesisches Bild*)
Still fairly widespread, this pack is used for playing the German games of Skat, Schafkopf and Doppelkopf. Size of cards is about 100mm × 55mm, and

19. Prussian pattern: King of Acorns and Ober of Leaves

20. Prussian pattern: two Polish versions; King of Bells and Deuce of Hearts

packs contain 32 cards. Each suit consists of King, Ober, Unter, numerical cards 10–7 and Deuce. Modern packs are double-ended, but older packs show single-ended court and numerical cards.

Modern Prussian packs are easy to recognise, since all the numerical cards bear illustrations of German towns and buildings. This was also a feature of other regional packs, but the Prussian pack alone includes the names of the places illustrated. Prussia, as a region, of course, no longer exists politically, yet the cards continue to illustrate places which were once in the German province, including

Danzig and Breslau, which now belong to Poland.

The Kings of the Prussian pack bear a suitmark on each side of their head, while the Deuces all show female figures, apparently doing duty as Queens. The design of the pack marketed today by Vereinigte Altenburger und Stralsunder Spielkartenfabriken AG (ASS) still has a charming nineteenth-century appearance, although it has obviously been redrawn to suit modern production methods. The Seven of Bells, for instance, shows the Company's factory at Stuttgart. ASS have instituted the important Deutsches Spielkarten-Museum there.

The pack marketed by another German firm, F. X. Schmid Vereinigte Münchener Spielkarten-Fabriken KG, is rather more modern in design, and the towns and buildings illustrated are different.

Characteristics of the courts in the pack are, on the suit of Leaves, the pipe-smoking Ober, the Unter with the dead bird, and the girl hunter with her bow and arrow shown on the Deuce. On the Hearts suit, the Deuce figure is somewhat reminiscent of the national Germania figure, the Ober carries a shotgun, and the Unter a bottle of champagne. On the Acorns suit, the Deuce is represented by a figure which sometimes looks like a plump boy, but at other times is undoubtedly a girl. He (or she) holds a stick with a bunch of grapes in the right hand, and a goblet in the left. The unbearded Ober holds a small long-handled hatchet or halberd. On the suit of Bells, the Deuce shows a husky young woman with a cornucopia of flowers, sometimes holding a scroll inscribed *Deutsche Karte*, the Ober holds a cigar in one hand and a cane in the other. The Unter holds a glass in one hand and a slate with a number on it in the other.

As the name implies, the Prussian-Silesian pattern was used in the district of Silesia, which is now under Polish rule. After the end of World War II, the Poles continued to produce a version of the Prussian pattern. Apparently, it is still popular, for

PLATE 8

A. Historical pack by VSS, Altenburg; B. 'Renovation 2000' by ASS; C. 'Tudor Rose' by Piatnik; D. 'Versailles' by Grimaud; E. 'Napoleon' by Catel & Farcy; F. 'Napoleone' by Stampati Arienti, Lissone; G. 'World Bridge' by Modiano; H. Bible pack for El Al Airlines, by Piatnik, for Lion Playing Card Co; J. 'Civilizaciones' by Fournier; K. 'Fortune Wheel' by Piatnik.

the Polish playing-card enterprise (KZWP) has produced a new design. This modern, attractive version still retains the German suits, but the pack has been given a new look.

The girl hunter is retained on the Deuce of Leaves, while the King of Leaves holds a scroll as well as his mace. The hunting theme is maintained with the Ober holding an old-fashioned shotgun. The Unter, however, is holding bunches of grapes, while on Hearts, the Amazonian female remains on the Deuce. The King holds an orb and a sword, the Ober has a crossbow, and the Unter holds a jug and beaker. With the exception of the Deuce, which portrays a very queenly female, the rest of the Bells suit has an oriental appearance, with the Ober using a bow and arrow and the Unter holding a hawk by a chain. The Acorns suit has a seventeenth-century look; the Deuce retains the young child figure, undoubtedly a boy in this case, with the Ober looking like a Spanish soldier and the Unter a minstrel.

The numerical cards, which run from 10 to 7 in each suit, show vignetted pictures of modern Polish cities. Some of the former Prussian cities appear, but with the present Polish names, such as Wroclaw (Breslau) on the Nine of Bells; Olsztyn (Allenstein) on the Ten of Bells; Szczecin (Stettin) on the Eight of Bells; Walbrzych (Waldenberg) on the Ten of Acorns; Opole (Oppeln) on the Seven of Acorns, and Gdansk (Danzig) on the Ten of Hearts.

The pack, as used today in Poland, still uses certain terms borrowed from the old German pack. In Silesia, the Bells suit is called *Szele* (pronounced *sheller*), from German *Schellen*, and the Unter is often referred to as *Bubek*, from German *Bube*. The highest-valued card in the pack is the Deuce, known in Poland as *Dama* (or Queen). Next comes the King (or *Król*), the Ober (or *Wyznik*), and the Unter (or *Niznik*, sometimes called *Bubek*). The Deuce of Acorns, with its boy-figure, is valued highest of all.

Württemberg-Palatine pattern (*Württembergisch-Pfälzisches Bild*)

This is another of the existing German regional patterns, and it is used, with 36 cards to the pack, for playing a game called 'Tarock', not to be confused with games played with proper Tarot cards. For the games of Gaigel and Binokel, two identical packs of 24 cards are used. Thirty-six-card packs consist of King, Ober, Unter, Deuce and numerical cards

21. Württemberg pattern: King of Bells and Ober of Leaves

10–6, while the only numerical cards in 24-card packs are the Ten and Seven. Size of cards is about 100mm × 55mm, all being double-ended.

The word *Ober* is usually printed on each end of those court-cards, with the figure shown mounted on a horse, while the Deuces are shown as follows: Bells, a vase surrounded by flowers and fruit;

COLOUR PLATE 3
A. The King of Clubs from a pack made for the Netherlands c1890 by Dondorf of Frankfurt.
B. A Swiss costume pack from Wüst of Frankfurt, made c1890. This King of Hearts shows men from Zug and St Gallen.
C. A pack from World War I, made in Altenburg c1917. The Jack of Clubs depicts the Field Marshal von Hindenburg.
D. The Jack of Hearts from a colourful pack made c1880 by Dondorf of Frankfurt.
E. Another Dondorf pack made c1930. This has a hunting theme, and the Queen of Spades shows a woman forest-dweller.
F. The Jack of Spades from a regional-costume pack made in Germany c1938.
G. The King of Spades represented by Julius Caesar in a Shakespearean pack made by Goodall of England c1900.
H. The Jack of Diamonds from a pack made in 1900 featuring actors from the Vienna Burgtheater.
J. An Austrian pack, known as the 'Gentleman Whist' pack, made in 1900 in honour of the Jubilee of the Emperor Franz Josef.

A

B

C

D

E

F

G

H

J

Leaves, crossed wine-bottles and a goblet; Hearts, bottles and glasses; and Acorns, a steaming punch-bowl. As with some other German regional packs, the Deuces are regarded as Aces, and sometimes marked with the index letter A.

Bavarian pattern (Bayrisches Bild)
The current design of the Bavarian pattern pack has double-ended courts, as well as double-ended numerical cards. Single-ended packs show illustrations at the bottom of all numerical cards. These designs include town and country scenes, and peasants at work and play.

There are 36 cards to a pack, which is used for playing the games of Tarock and Schafkopf, the composition being King, Ober, Unter and numerical cards 10–6 in each suit. The size of the cards is about 100mm × 55mm. Deuces are sometimes index-lettered A. On the Leaves suit, the Deuce shows a fancy vase containing flowers, the Ober plays a drum, while the Unter plays the flute. On the Acorns suit, the Deuce shows a naked small boy flourishing a tankard, while the Ober carries a shield. The Deuce of Hearts shows a Cupid inside an oval or round frame, while the Deuce of Bells shows a dog attacking a boar. The Unter of Bells flourishes

COLOUR PLATE 4
A. An advertising pack by Česká Grafická Unie of Prague. Made c1930 to advertise a nuts and bolts factory, this card represents the King of Leaves.
B. Another Czech pack, called 'Animal Skat'. Made by the same firm c1925, this card is the Ober of Acorns.
C. The Ober of Acorns from a non-standard Dondorf pack of c1910.
D. The Ober of Leaves from a German pack made during World War I. The pack was intended to acclaim the German war effort.
E. The King of Bells from a non-standard Dondorf pack of c1925.
F. The Unter of Acorns from a German historical pack of c1872, made by J. C. Jegel.
G. The Unter of Bells from a calendar pack made by Stefan Giergl of Pesth, Hungary, c1864.
H. A modern reprint of a patriotic pack designed by Hofmann in Czechoslovakia, 1920. The King of Bells shows Otakar II. Made by Piatnik of Vienna.
J. The Ober of Bells from a German pack of which a special printing was recently made. Cards show scenes of miners and salt mines near Bad Reichenhall.

22. Bavarian pattern: King of Hearts and Ober of Acorns

23. Salzburg pattern: King of Bells and Ober of Acorns

a sabre above his head. In older packs, the German tax stamp appears on the Deuce of Hearts.

Salzburg pattern (Salzburger Bild)
This is an Austrian version of the Bavarian pattern, but unlike its German counterpart is found only single-ended. The pack contains either 36 or 32 cards, about 100mm × 55mm in size. Suits consist of King, Ober, Unter, Deuce and numerical cards 10–7, the Seven being omitted for 32-card packs. Index-letters and figures do not appear.

Kings are all seated upon thrones, with all except the Leaves suit showing a shield. The shield of the King of Acorns shows a Cupid; that of the King of Hearts an Anchor, while the King of Bells's shield bears the arms of Salzburg. The Kings are all full-faced except the King of Leaves, who is in profile and looking to his right.

The rest of the court-cards include the following characteristics: Ober of Acorns carries an oval shield in his left hand and a drawn sword in his right; the Unter of Acorns carries a drawn sword in his right hand; the Ober of Leaves is a drummer; the Unter of Leaves is a flute-player; the Ober of Hearts has a sheathed sword on his left and holds a lance with both hands; the Ober of Bells holds his scabbard in his left hand and draws the sword with his right, while the Unter of Bells flourishes a drawn sword over his head. The Deuces show: Acorns, a young boy as Bacchus holding a glass and sitting astride a cask; Leaves, an Owl, Hart and Unicorn placed as heraldic supporters; Hearts, a blindfolded Cupid in an oval frame surmounted by a basket containing leaves; and Bells, a Boar.

The numerical cards all bear small vignetted pictures. These are usually as follows: Acorns has, on the Ten, a peasant sitting smoking; on the Nine, a traveller with his dog, sitting on a tree-trunk; Eight has a hunter accompanied by a dog and holding a hawk on a lead; Seven has a reveller with a glass of wine and a bottle; Six shows a peasant girl carrying a sheaf of corn and a rake. The Leaves suit shows: on the Ten, a hunter with his gun and three dogs; Nine, a youth with a sheep; Eight, a peasant couple talking; Seven, an angler and his wife; Six, a vase of flowers. On Hearts: Ten, two peasant girls talking; Nine, a peasant couple, one carrying a tub, and the other a stick; Eight, an elephant; Seven, a snake; and Six, a lion. On Bells: Ten, a shepherd with two sheep, blowing upon a horn; Nine, a man sitting

upon a tree-trunk receiving a beehive from a peasant girl; Eight, a traveller looking at the way ahead; Seven, a peasant girl with a goat; and Six, a tomb. The last-named card, the Six of Bells, also carries the single suitmarks for Acorns and Hearts, while at the top of the card is the word WELI. The reason for the inclusion of this word is not clear, except that it is the Turkish word for the tomb of a saint, while the illustration clearly shows a tomb.

Franconian pattern (*Fränkisches Bild*)

Franconia, as a state, has long since ceased to exist, but this regional pattern of German cards continues to be produced under this name. Modern packs are all double-ended, but older packs can be found with single-ended cards. Size of cards is about 100mm × 55mm. The packs consist of either 32 or 36 cards, consisting of King, Ober, Unter, Deuce (sometimes index-lettered A), and numerical cards 10–6 in each suit. Sixes are omitted for the shorter packs. The Franconian pattern obviously has some affinity with the Bavarian pattern, as there are many points of similarity.

All the Knaves, except those of Leaves, bear arms. The Ober of Acorns carries a sword, and the Unter a pike; the Ober of Hearts has a long lance, disappearing out of the picture, while the Unter has an axe. Both the Knaves of Bells carry swords, but the Knaves of the Leaves suit play a drum and a flute.

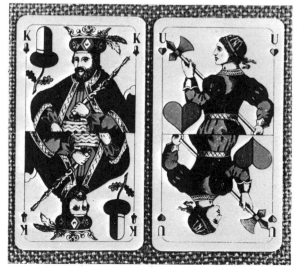

24. Franconian pattern: King of Acorns and Unter of Hearts

The Deuces show: Acorns, a heraldic lion; Hearts, two cornucopia of flowers; Leaves, an eagle holding an orb; and Bells, little more than the plain suitmarks.

Bohemian or Prague pattern (Böhmisch-Deutsches Bild, or Präger Bild)

This is, in effect, a Czech version of the Franconian pattern, which is still being made by the Czechoslovak playing-card enterprise, Obchodní Tiskárny np Kolín (OTK). There are 32 cards to the pack, which consists of King, Ober, Unter, Deuce and numerical cards 10–7 in each suit. The cards are

25. Bohemian pattern: King of Bells and Deuce of Acorns

26. Saxon pattern: King of Leaves and Deuce of Hearts

single-ended, not indexed, and measure about 105mm × 63mm.

The design of this pack appears to date back earlier than that of the present Franconian pack. Each King is seated upon a throne, with a suitmark at each side of the head, the crown having a somewhat oriental appearance. The Knaves of Acorns both carry a sword in each hand; those of Leaves show a drummer and a flute-player (cf the Bavarian pattern); Hearts show the Knaves carrying long staves; and Bells has each Knave wielding a sword.

Numerical cards bear small vignetted pictures; those on the suit of Acorns usually being as follows: Ten, no picture; Nine, a transfixed bird; Eight, a shepherd with a sheep, blowing upon a horn (cf the Ten of Bells in the Salzburg pattern); Seven, a peasant with a pipe and walking-stick. On Leaves: Ten, a dog; Nine, a goat; Eight, an elephant; Seven, a man with a sword; on Hearts: Ten, a Cupid shooting an arrow into a heart; Nine, a narrow-based pyramid; Eight, a fountain; Seven, a tree growing in a tub; on Bells: Ten, two musicians and a performing bear; Nine, a horse tethered to a stake; Eight, a dog, and also the maker's imprint; and Seven, a flower growing in a tub.

Saxon pattern (Sächsisches Bild, Thüringisches Bild, or occasionally, Chemnitzer Bild)

This is another surviving German regional pattern. Saxon-pattern packs contain either 32 or 36 cards: King, Ober, Unter, Deuce, and numerical cards 10–7 or 10–6 in each suit. A suitmark appears on either side of the head of each King, and the Unters of Leaves and Acorns hold stalks supporting the suitmark. Sometimes the Unter of Bells has a bird perched upon his wrist, although many modern packs have omitted this last feature from the design. The size of the cards is about 100mm × 55mm.

On the Deuces appear: Bells, a courting couple being watched by a third party; Leaves, the coat of

PLATE 10
A. 'Simpson's of Piccadilly' publicity pack by De La Rue; B. 'Comedia' by Öberg; C. Icelandic mythological pack by Sigurlinna Petursson; D. 'Picart le Doux' by De La Rue; E. 'Classic' by Fournier; F. 'Scaramouche' by Triboulet; G. 'Jeu des Peintres' by Grimaud; H. 'Hannelore Heise' essay by VEB Altenburg; J. Bridge pack for Banque Nationale de Paris by Van Genechten.

A

B

C

D

E

F

G

H

J

arms of Saxony; Acorns, a bear's, or a lion's head, above which is a scroll inscribed *Schwerdter-Karte*, or *Feinste Doppelbilder Karte*; and on Hearts, the maker's imprint, surmounted by a basket of flowers.

Before World War II, the Altenburg playing-card firm put out a local variation of the Saxon pattern known as the Altenburg pattern (*Altenburger Einfachbild*). However, apart from showing a bear instead of a lion on the Deuce of Acorns, it varies but little. Since the war, too, Saxon-pattern packs have been made by West German makers, and also by the East German card-making enterprise, Altenburger Spielkartenfabrik. This last-named firm maintains a fine museum devoted to playing-cards. Another minor variety was the *Brunner*, made by Glanz of Vienna in 1832.

Hungarian pattern (*Ungarisches Bild*); *also 'Seasons' pattern*

This pack is a survivor of the Austro-Hungarian Empire, and versions are still made in Austria, Hungary and Czechoslovakia. Full packs contain 36 cards (King, Ober, Unter, Deuce and numerical cards 10–6 in each suit). Reduced packs are also sold containing 32 or even 24 cards, when Sixes, or even Sixes, Sevens and Eights, are omitted. Courts are not normally indexed, but the numerical cards bear Roman numbers. Packs, which are double-ended, are found in three basic sizes: about 120mm × 75mm; 100mm × 60mm; and a patience size of 67mm × 43mm.

This pack is sometimes called the Seasons pattern because the Deuces show scenes depicting the four seasons. The seasons are named on the cards in German, Hungarian or English, although the packs made in Czechoslovakia nowadays have dropped the titles altogether.

The scenes shown on the Deuces are: on Bells, summer (*Sommer* or *Nyár*), with a peasant resting and holding a scythe; on Acorns, winter (*Winter* or *Tél*), with a peasant warming himself by a fire; on Leaves, autumn (*Herbst* or *Ösz*), with a peasant helping himself to a drink from a tub; and on Hearts, spring (*Frühling* or *Tavasz*), with a peasant girl picking flowers.

Yet another name for this pack is the 'Tell' pattern, from its use of named characters from the well-known Swiss legend of William Tell. Despite this, the pack has no connection with Switzerland,

27. Hungarian pattern: Class A. Ober of Hearts and Deuce of Leaves

28. Hungarian pattern: Class B. Ober of Hearts and Deuce of Leaves

and seems to have originated in Hungary during the early part of the nineteenth century. The earliest example known was made about 1835 by József Schneider of Pesth.

The designs of the Kings and Deuces were known on earlier packs, but the Tell designs, as shown on the Knaves, were adopted, not from the Swiss legend itself, but from characters in Schiller's play, *Wilhelm Tell*, which was first performed in Hungarian in 1833. Although the first 'Tell' designs appeared at least as early as 1835, few packs are known which were issued before 1865; since then the cards appear to have been in popular use.

Hungarian pattern packs fall into two basic classes: (a) Hungarian proper, and (b) Austro-Czech. Class (a) is identified by having Deuces as described above, while class (b) has the following variations on the Deuces:

On Bells: (summer) is a peasant girl holding a sickle and a sheaf of corn; on Acorns: (winter) is an old peasant woman carrying faggots and using a staff; on Leaves: (autumn) are two peasant boys busy pressing grapes; and on Hearts: a peasant girl holding a basket of flowers. There is also some variation in the design of the Knaves and numerical cards.

As with some other German and Austrian packs, the Six of Bells also carries the suitmarks for Acorns and Hearts, with the word WELI at the top. Most of the numerical cards show small vignetted pictures of country scenes.

The named characters shown on the Knave cards are: Ober of Bells, *Itell Reding* (*Reding Itell*); Unter of Bells, *Stüssi d. Flurschütz* (*Stüszi vadasz*, ie Stussi the Hunter); Ober of Acorns, *Wilhelm Tell* (*Tell Vilmos*); Unter of Acorns, *Rudolf Harras* (*Harras Rudolf*); Ober of Leaves, *Walter Fürst* (*Fürst Walter*); Unter of Leaves, *Ulrich Rudenz* (*Rudenz Ulrich*); Ober of Hearts, *Hermann Gessler* (*Geszler H.*); and Unter of Hearts, *Kuoni d. Hirt* (*Kuoni pásztor*, or Kuoni the shepherd).

The Austrian card-making firm of Ferdinand Piatnik used to maintain a factory in Budapest, but after World War II, it was taken over by the Hungarian state. However, the enterprise, which operates under the title Játékkártyagyár, celebrated the 100th anniversary of the factory in 1969 by issuing a special modern version of the Hungarian pattern pack.

New Altenburg pattern (Neues Altenburger Bild)
Although using German suits, this is not a traditional pack at all, having been designed quite

29. New Altenburg pattern: King of Acorns and Deuce of Hearts

recently at the East German firm at Altenburg. However, since it appears to have been introduced quite deliberately to replace the traditional designs, it is logical to rank it as a standard German pattern.

The pack is used for the game of Skat, and therefore employs 32 cards. Influenced, no doubt, by the more common French-suited cards, the court-cards are now shown as King, Queen, Jack, Deuce and 10–7 numerical cards. All are indexed except the Deuces, following the standard German letters as for French-suited packs: K, D, B, 10 etc.

The design of the court-cards has doubtless been influenced by the Berliner French-suited pack, but the Deuces bear the following characteristics: Bells, an ermine cloak draped around a shield with an overturned crown above; Acorns, a blue cloth draped around a shield with a helmet above; Leaves, two swords on a red cloth surmounted by a helmet; and Hearts, a mediaeval pair of war-clubs beneath a red and yellow cloth draped around a shield, surmounted by a Papal crown. The words *Altenburger Spielkarte* appear on a tablet at the centre. All cards are double-ended.

SWISS CARDS

Although within the general sphere of German-type cards, Switzerland has developed its own variant of the German suits. Hearts and Leaves have been displaced in favour of two local suits: Shields and Flowers. The four Swiss suits are therefore: Shields (*Schilde*); Flowers or Roses (*Rosen*); Acorns

(*Eicheln*); and Bells (*Schellen*).

Swiss-suited packs, called *Jasskarten*, contain 36 cards, each suit consisting of King, Ober, Unter (called *Under* in Switzerland); Deuce, numerical cards from 9–6, and a card known as the Banner, once used also in German packs. Until recently, both

30. Swiss pattern: King of Shields and Banner of Flowers

single- and double-ended packs were available, but production of single-ended packs has now ceased.

The cards are often not indexed, but the three court-cards and the Banner are marked for identification as *König*, *Ober*, *Under*, and a symbol representing the roman numeral X.

The Banner, in fact, represents the old numerical card for Ten, but bears only one suitmark, which is shown on a pennant-type flag, hence its name. Even modern Swiss cards have a somewhat primitive look, particularly noticeable on the single-ended packs, since the old designs have been preserved over the centuries.

All Kings on single-ended cards, with the exception of the King of Flowers, are shown seated on thrones. The Obers of Acorns and Bells smoke pipes, as does the *Under* of Flowers. The *Under* of Bells looks like a court jester, and the *Under* of Shields holds a sealed envelope, and has a quill pen in his mouth. The only bearded figure on the single-ended cards is the King of Acorns, all other courts showing clean-shaven figures.

Double-ended packs have slightly more up-to-date looking designs. The pipe-smokers are now the *Under* of Flowers, the Ober and *Under* of Bells, the Ober of Shields, and the Ober of Acorns. The *Under* of Shields carries an envelope, and has a quill pen tucked behind his ear. The bearded King of Acorns is joined by a bearded and moustached King of Bells.

The cards are about 86mm × 56mm in size, although recently a patience-sized pack was introduced bearing new, rather modernistic designs. The Deuces of Shields and Bells usually show the maker's name and his address. Most double-ended packs have numerical cards showing indices in the corners.

6
FRENCH-SUITED PLAYING-CARDS: WITHIN FRANCE

The first evidence we have of the existence of playing-cards in France is found in the records of Laurent Aycardi, a notary of Marseilles, who refers to them in an entry dated 30 August 1381. In the following year, the magistrate of Lille issued a decree forbidding their use. Only seventy years later, however, it seems that the legislation against the use of cards was withdrawn, for by this time French card-makers were using wood-blocks for printing.

As in Italy and Germany, with the spread of card-playing makers established themselves in various parts of the country, and a national suit-system for French cards emerged. These suitmarks first appeared some time in the early part of the fifteenth century.

German card-makers had reigned supreme in Europe, exporting their products to many parts, but by the middle of the fifteenth century, a home industry had been established in France, and the familiar Hearts, Clubs, Diamonds and Spades made their appearance. Owing to their simplicity the French suitmarks soon became popular, and other suitmarks from Italy and Germany began to fall from favour.

It seems probable that the French symbols were derived from the German: since Hearts already existed, Clubs could have been an adaptation of Acorns, and Spades could easily have been derived from the Leaves suit. In France, the names of the suits were, and remain, *Coeurs* (Hearts); *Trèfles* (Trefoils, but known in England as Clubs); *Piques* (Pikes, but English usage made them Spades); and *Carreaux* (actually small squares, but called Diamonds by English players).

During the fifteenth and sixteenth centuries, France overtook Germany as a card-manufacturing country, and soon became the main producer, exporting to England, Italy, Spain, the Low Countries and Switzerland.

Regional French patterns of packs began to emerge at a very early date, until about ten recognisable types were established. Up to 1701 it had been possible to produce new and fanciful designs, but in that year, the nine regional patterns were established by law. These continued their existence until 1780, when all regional patterns, except for that of Paris, were swept away, and for the next thirteen years, the only official design for French playing-cards was the Paris pattern. No changes were made until 1793, when a decree from the Revolutionary government forbade the use of royal emblems on cards. This resulted in such crudities as the crowns being cut from the wood-blocks used for printing, but eventually, new designs were made, showing the figures of the courts without crowns.

Later, a completely new design appeared, in which Kings were replaced by 'Sages', 'Elements' or 'Geniuses'; Queens were turned into 'Virtues', 'Liberties' or 'Seasons', and the Jacks were displaced by 'Egalities', 'Heroes' or 'Cultivators'. Such innovations were never popular, and with the return of France to monarchy, the old Paris pattern was revived.

Regional patterns of France were as follows:

Paris pattern (Portrait de Paris)
The best known, and most widely-spread of French regional patterns, this became established by the seventeenth century (after earlier variations) in a wide area in and around the French capital. After the French Revolution, the Paris pattern was re-drawn, and in 1813 the design, more or less as used today, was introduced. The only changes since that time have been the addition of indices and the introduction of double-ended cards during the early nineteenth century.

A special feature of the Paris pattern is the employment of names for each court-card. Other regional patterns also adopted this feature, but the Paris pattern has been consistent in always using the same names, which are still in use today. Main features of the Paris pattern are:

Hearts: The King carries a sword in his right hand, and an orb bearing the cross of Lorraine in the other. On modern cards, this orb is not seen, since it is obscured by the diagonal division on court-cards to form the double-ended design. The figure of the King is believed to represent Charlemagne, and is named on the card as *Charles*. The Queen of Hearts is named *Judith*, or, on early cards, *Judic*. The Jack of Hearts, named *Lahire*, is seen full-face.

Clubs: The King, named *Alexandre*, is accompanied by a small animal which looks like a lion, but this disappears in double-ended packs. He holds a sceptre in his right hand. The Queen, named *Argine* (an anagram of *Regina*), unlike her sisters, bears no flower, but holds a fan in her left hand, although this is not seen in double-ended packs. The Jack of Clubs (*Lancelot*), holds a halberd in his left hand and a ribbon with a shield attached in his right. The shield frequently bears the name of the card-maker. On double-ended cards, the halberd disappears.

Diamonds: The King is named *Cézar*, and is seen in profile, looking towards his left. He holds a sceptre in his left hand, and a shell-shaped shield appears below his belt. On double-ended cards, the sceptre disappears, and the shield can only be seen partially. The Queen (*Rachel*) still has her flower on double-ended cards, although her hand cannot be seen. The Jack of Diamonds (*Hector*), holds a halberd in his left hand, invisible on double-ended cards.

Spades: The King (*David*) holds a sceptre in his right hand, and rests it on a lyre or harp. The Queen of Spades (*Pallas*), bears a shield on her robes, and holds a flower in her right hand. The Jack (*Hogier*) is accompanied by a small dog, wears a hat with a feather, and holds a halberd in his left hand. All this

31. Paris pattern: King of Hearts and Queen of Clubs

detail, except for the feather, is not shown on double-ended cards.

Paris-pattern packs usually contain 52 cards, with the customary addition of extra cards, such as jokers. Size is commonly about 85mm × 55mm.

Lyons pattern (*Portrait de Lyon*)

Up to the seventeenth century, there were several minor variations of the Lyons pattern, since makers were exporting to a number of countries, and requirements varied. Main destinations were the various German states, Switzerland, Italy and Spain. By the seventeenth century, the design had been stabilised to a pack with the following characteristics:

Each of the Kings bears a sceptre surmounted by a fleur-de-lis, and the King of Hearts, who bears his

32. Lyons pattern: King of Spades and Jack of Spades

sceptre in his right hand, supports a hawk or parrot in his left. The King of Clubs also carries an orb. Before the middle of the eighteenth century, the Queens of Hearts and Clubs carried a sceptre, but this was replaced by flowers and fans, carried also by the other two Queens. At one time, the Queens of Diamonds and Clubs were accompanied by the motto *Mais bien vous*. The Jack of Spades is shown smoking a pipe, and carrying an axe which shows the initials of the maker. The Jack of Clubs is shown carrying a shield.

Dauphiné pattern (*Portrait du Dauphiné*)

This pattern was known in the sixteenth century, and was in use for at least 200 years after that time. The King of Clubs bears an orb in one hand and a sword in the other, and the King of Diamonds supports a hawk in one hand. The Jacks are most distinctive in this pack, with the Jack of Hearts wearing armour and a close-fitting cap with a tassel. He is bare-foot, his right hand holds a drawn sword, and he holds his other hand up, with index finger extended.

The Jack of Diamonds, wearing similar clothes, is seen in profile, walking towards his left. His boots – or rather spats, since there seem to be no feet in them – are adorned with what looks like a human mask. He carries a stick or baton in his right hand. The Jack of Clubs stands face-on, with his hand on his hip, supporting a halberd with the other. He wears

34. Provence pattern: King and Queen of Hearts

knee-breeches and carries a sword. The Jack of Spades is also seen full-face, supporting a halberd with his right hand and carrying a short sword in the other. He wears a jerkin to the knees, a plumed hat, and knee-boots. A scroll bearing the maker's name is entwined between his legs.

Provence pattern (*Portrait de Provence*)

There are examples of playing-cards with the Provence pattern dating back to the end of the fifteenth century. By the seventeenth century, the pattern was well established, and it did not change until 1780, when the Paris pattern was imposed on all France. Some details of the design are:

The King of Hearts carries a crowned hawk or falcon in his hand, while the Queen wears a kind of armour of scales, which can be seen on her arms and legs. During the fifteenth century, the Queen was shown wearing animal skins and furs as *la belle sauvage*. The Jack of Hearts is seen full-face, one hand on his hip and the other holding a halberd.

The King of Clubs is armed with an axe, on the blade of which is shown a fleur-de-lis pattern; the Queen holds a sunflower, and the Jack of Clubs wears his hair in close plaits. A scroll bearing the

33. Dauphiné pattern: Jack of Hearts and Jack of Diamonds

PLATE 12
A. 'Bourbon Bridge' by Müller; B. 'Hector de Trois' by Grimaud; C. Lyons pack facsimile, by Scolar Press; D. Fluorescent pack by Héron; E. Literary pack No 2926; F. Costume pack No 2901; G.–H. Slavic pack No 2900; J. Rococo pack No 2901. Packs E–J by GKM, Leningrad.

A

B

C

D

E

F

G

H

J

name of the maker is interwoven between his legs.

The King of Diamonds carries a very thin sceptre ending with a large ornament. His Queen wears a dress with enormous cylindrical sleeves, which, viewed from the front, look like a very large bow. The Jack is seen with his back to us, and is wearing a jacket with large sleeves and a hat resembling a turban.

The King of Spades is seen in profile facing right, bearing his sceptre on his shoulder. Similarly to the Queen of Clubs the Queen carries a sunflower, while the Jack is attired like that of Clubs, with plaited hair and the maker's scroll between his feet.

Burgundy or Lorraine pattern (Portrait de Bourgogne, or Portrait de Lorraine)

This pack was originally made by card-makers in Lyons for export to Burgundy during the seventeenth century. It was also sent to Flanders and Lorraine, and became known as La Plume à Chapeau, from the peculiarity of the design of the Jack of Clubs, who is shown with a helmet bearing a very large feather.

The design was copied by makers in Dijon, Besançon and Salins, and was in use in Lorraine, with minor variations, until 1751, when it was replaced by the Paris pattern. A rather better-produced version was made for export. Main features of the design are:

The Kings all wear large crowns, with the King of Clubs carrying a sceptre, and the King of Hearts wearing a kind of badge bearing his suitmark. He carries his sceptre on his shoulder. Except for the Queen of Diamonds, the Queens carry flowers. Of the Jacks, that of Hearts is seen full-face, holding a sword in his right hand and a halberd in the left.

The Jack of Spades has plaited hair (as in the Provence pattern) and holds a sword and halberd. The name of the maker appears beneath his feet. The helmet of the Jack of Clubs carries the large feather described above, while the name of the maker usually appears at his feet.

Auvergne pattern (Portrait d'Auvergne)

One of the very early French regional patterns, that of Auvergne had acquired certain recognisable characteristics by the seventeenth century, later versions sometimes using the same names as the Paris pattern. Main centres of manufacture were Thiers,

35. Burgundy pattern: King of Hearts and Jack of Clubs

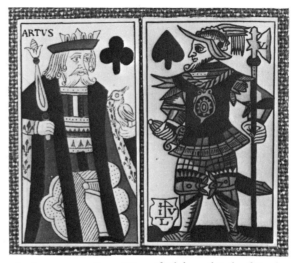

36. Auvergne pattern: King of Clubs and Jack of Spades

Puy and Clermont. Principal features of the design are:

The King of Hearts carries a sword in his left hand, and an orb in his right; the other Kings all carry sceptres. The King of Diamonds has his sceptre in the left hand, the others in the right. The King of Clubs carries a small hawk or falcon in his left hand.

The Queens all carry a sceptre and a flower, except for the Queen of Spades who holds a small dog in her right hand. The Queens of Clubs and Diamonds carry their sceptres in their right hands and look towards their left, while the other two hold their sceptres in their left hands and look towards their right.

50

The Jacks all have plumed helmets and wear the armour of knights. Each has one hand holding a halberd, and the other on the hilt of his sword. All are shown in profile, those of Diamonds and Clubs looking to their left and the other two looking to their right. The name of the maker usually appears at the bottom of the design of the Jack cards.

Limousin pattern (*Portrait du Limousin*)

This is little more than a copy, in smaller form, of the Auvergne pattern, but rather less well executed. It was in use at Limoges, Angoulême and Poitiers. One small difference is that all Jacks face to their right.

Guyenne pattern (*Portrait de Guyenne*)

Until 1716, the card-makers of Guyenne more or less copied the export version of the Auvergne pattern, making a few minor alterations in the design. After that time, the cards became slightly smaller, but the figures upon them were not reduced in proportion, thus making them appear rather large in comparison with the dimensions of the card. By the middle of the eighteenth century, the following features in the design had emerged:

The King of Hearts carries, instead of a sceptre, a baton supporting a large fleur-de-lis on a triangular base. He holds a harp or lyre in his right hand. The King of Clubs holds a sceptre in his left hand. One end of it terminates in a heart, but the top ends in a vessel emitting flames. The King of Diamonds holds in his left hand a sceptre, ornamented by a heart surmounted by an eye. The King of Spades holds an axe, and all the Queens carry flowers. Except for the Queen of Hearts, who is seen in profile looking to her left, the Queens appear full-face. The Jacks all have very wide sleeves to their jackets, particularly those of Hearts and Diamonds. The Jack of Clubs has plaited hair, and holds a spear with a large blade. The Jack of Spades has his hand upon his hip, and holds a halberd in his right hand. Jacks are shown in profile and looking to their left, except for Jack of Spades, who is full-face. Both he and the Jack of Clubs wear knee-breeches, while the others wear jerkins or jackets reaching to the knee.

Languedoc pattern (*Portrait du Languedoc*)

This is really an adaptation of the Guyenne pattern, but generally better drawn, and intended for export.

37. Limousin pattern: King of Clubs and Jack of Spades

38. Guyenne pattern: King of Diamonds and Jack of Spades

39. Languedoc pattern: King of Diamonds and Jack of Spades

51

The cards are smaller, and were made at Toulouse, Carcassonne, Béziers and Albi. A distinguishing detail of the design is that the King of Diamonds holds a bag in his right hand. In the other hand he holds a sceptre surmounted by a crescent. With the Guyenne pattern, a shield normally occupies this position.

Rouen pattern No 1 (*Portrait de Rouen*)

This pattern, which is not one of the nine regional *portraits* which later became legally acceptable, is

40. Rouen pattern No 1: Queen of Clubs and Jack of Diamonds

41. Rouen pattern No 2: King of Diamonds and Jack of Spades

called here 'No 1' to distinguish it from the later pattern described below. Rouen was regarded as being within the area of the Paris pattern, although the numerous makers there produced other designs. This particular pattern dates from the earlier half of the sixteenth century, but disappeared something over a hundred years later. A double-ended version appeared about 1780.

One pack which has survived was made by Charles Dubois. The cards are very narrow, 43mm across, and nearly twice as deep. The pack was probably intended for export to the German-speaking countries, since a double-headed eagle appears on the shields of the Kings of Hearts and Diamonds.

The Jacks, too, have a somewhat Teutonic look, while the courts of the pack have distinctive names:

Hearts: King, *Jullius Cézar*; Queen, *Héleine*; Jack, *Siprien Roman*

Clubs: King, *Hector*; Queen, *Pentaxlée*; Jack, *Capitane Taillant*

Diamonds: King, *Charles*; Queen, *Thérèse*; Jack, *Capita Fily*

Spades: King, *David*; Queen, *Bersabée*; Jack, no name, except for scroll of the maker, Charles Dubois

Three of the Kings hold shields, and the fourth, the King of Spades, holds a harp. Two of the Queens (Hearts and Clubs) hold flowers, and the other two, sceptres. Two of the Jacks (Diamonds and Clubs) wear knee-breeches, the others knee-length jerkins.

Rouen pattern No 2 (*Portrait de Rouen*)

Rouen card-makers were much employed in making cards for export, sending packs as far afield as Switzerland, Spain, Portugal, Flanders and England. With the coming of laws and restrictions on the trade, many card-makers left the town to settle in Holland, Germany and Belgium. By the eighteenth century, a number had also left to set up business in England, where cards had become well established.

It is generally accepted today that the original design from which the English pattern was derived came from Rouen, and this design is described here

PLATE 13
A. 'Brocades' publicity pack by Piatnik; B. 'Dodwell'; C. 'Sharp Oracle'; D. Edwards I; E. Edwards III; F. Crown II; G. 'Ukiyo-e'; H. Toyopet Crown; J. 'Young Men'. Packs B–J all by Nintendo, Japan.

under the title 'Rouen Pattern No 2'. The chief characteristics of the pattern are:

The King of Hearts brandishes an axe in his left hand, while the King of Diamonds, who is seen in profile, his head to his right, also holds an axe in his right hand. The King of Spades holds a sword upright in his left hand and an orb in his right, and the King of Clubs wields an upright sword in his left hand and an orb in his right.

The Queens all hold flowers in their left hands, but the only one to hold a sceptre is the Queen of Spades. The Jack of Hearts, seen in profile, his head to his left, holds a halberd in his left hand, and a sword, blade downwards, in his right. The Jack of Diamonds is seen full-face, with a halberd in his left hand, wearing a sword in a scabbard. The Jack of Spades has his back to us, while his head, in profile, looks to his right. He holds a halberd in his right hand, and the end of a sword-scabbard is just visible below his tunic. The Jack of Clubs, seen full-face, is glancing to his right, and carries a spear or lance in his right hand. This card usually carries the name of the maker on a scroll at the bottom.

7
FRENCH-SUITED PLAYING CARDS: OUTSIDE FRANCE

BRITAIN AND AMERICA

Playing-cards arrived in England by the mid-fifteenth century. No actual cards from this date have survived, but the earliest actual representation of an English playing-card appears in an eight-page pamphlet called *The Bloody Game at Cards* published about the year 1642. This is a satirical Royalist tract, but it does illustrate an early version of the King of Hearts.

Our knowledge of the existence of playing-cards before this date comes almost entirely from records of laws against them. A statute prohibiting them under the name 'Cardes a Juer' is dated 29 September 1464, and they are referred to in a letter written by Margery Paston to her husband, probably dated about 1484.

Henry VIII tried to suppress them in a proclamation dated May 1526, and the puritanical John Northbrooke of Bristol, wrote a sermon about 1576 condemning them:

> I say with good Father Saint Cyprian: The playe at Cardes is an invention of the Deuill, which he founde out that he might the easier bring in Ydolatrie amongst men. For the Kings and Coate cardes that we use nowe were in olde time the ymages of Idols and false Gods: which since they that woulde seeme Christians have changed into Charlemane, Launcelot, Hector, and such like names, because they would not seeme to imitate their ydolatrie herein, and yet maintaine the playe it self, the very inuention of Satan, the Deuill, and would disguise this mischief under the cloake of such gaye names.

Playing-cards were obviously familiar to Northbrooke, so we can take it that card-playing was widespread by that date. There are plenty of other allusions of the kind, but the earliest surviving

42. Origin of English pattern: Kings of Hearts from (*left*) Rouen pattern No 2 and (*right*) an early English design of about 1640

43. English pattern: King of Hearts made about 1750 and King of Diamonds from same date

44. English pattern: Jacks of Spades and Clubs made about 1750

45. English patterns: Queens of Hearts (*left*) from about 1750, and (*right*) about 1880.

examples of English playing-cards, now in the British Museum, date from 1590. Legislation against cards levied its toll, with the result that the products of over 250 years of English card-making have disappeared for ever.

English cards have used French suits right from the beginning, although a few packs from other countries had made their way into England, without apparently making much impact, apart from helping to give names to the English suits.

The pattern of the English pack can be traced back to a fifteenth-century ancestor made in Rouen, which is described under 'Rouen Pattern No 2'. The French have long since abandoned the design, but the Rouen card-makers no doubt found a ready market for their cards in England, where the pattern

was accepted, copied and used for 370 years.

The insular English, however, refused to adopt the French names for the suits, and instead, made up their own for some, like Diamonds, and adopted the Spanish name for Spades. Hearts is a translation of the French, and Clubs is a translation of the Spanish *bastos*.

An example of the Rouen pattern No 2 exists in a museum in that city, allowing a direct comparison with the English pattern as it has developed, and as it survives today.

An examination of English cards made at various periods will reveal that the basic design has changed but little, although the pattern has become more formalised and sophisticated. Some of the original detail has been lost, and some has been distorted by copyists and engravers through the centuries. Before the middle of the nineteenth century, playing-cards were single-ended, and it was possible to examine the detail of the design on the courts more closely. These are some of the main changes in detail:

In the original Rouen pattern, the King of Hearts wielded an axe in his left hand, but in the English pattern, the object held has been distorted so much that later engravers have assumed it to be the head of a sword, which is now shown instead. The King of Spades has lost his right hand, although it still remains in some early English packs. The King of Clubs still holds the sword and the orb, but the latter has changed in appearance. The Rouen King's orb was surmounted by the cross of Lorraine, whereas the English King's orb was changed to a simple cross, and then later to the fleur-de-lis motif which now adorns it. The fingers holding it have disappeared; and the King of Diamonds has lost the hand holding the axe. The Queen of Hearts, in double-ended packs has lost her right hand, although it did appear in the full-length version.

The Queen of Diamonds has also lost her right hand in double-ended packs, and is sometimes portrayed in the reverse position. The Queen of Spades remains the only Queen to hold a sceptre;

PLATE 14
A–D. Four cards from a 'transport' pack for the Industrial Bank of Japan; E. 'Suzuran-Maru'; F. Railways souvenir pack; G. 'Suntory' souvenir pack; H. 'Seiko Fashion'; J. African souvenir pack by Modiano. Packs A–H by Nintendo.

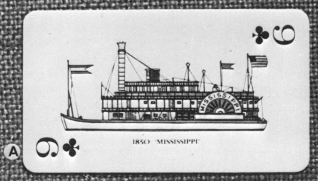

9 ♣ · 9 ♣

1850 'MISSISSIPPI'

A

A ♠ · A ♠

1898 PANHADET ET LEVASSOR

B

2 ♠ · 2 ♠

1829 'ROCKET'

C

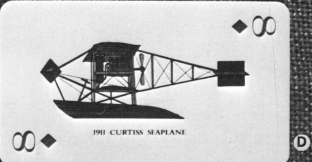

8 ♦ · 8 ♦

1911 CURTISS SEAPLANE

D

Q ♣ · Q ♣

E

H

K ♣ · K ♣

J ♣ · J ♣

Argentina National Railways Type 2 10 2

Q ♥

Q ♥

G

3 ♣ · 3 ♣

TURKANA WARRIOR

J

although the hand holding it has disappeared in double-ended packs. The Queen is sometimes shown, on modern packs, in the reverse position, that is, looking to her left, rather than to her right. The Queen of Clubs has also lost her right hand in double-headed packs, and she is also shown, like the Queens of Diamonds and Spades, occasionally in the reverse position.

The Jack of Hearts (also occasionally portrayed in the reverse position) has lost the hand which held the halberd, and his other hand no longer clutches the hilt of a sword. Nowadays he simply holds a small leaf in his fingers, an example of centuries of mis-drawing. The Jack of Diamonds still shows a hand holding the halberd, but his left hand, originally touching the scabbard, has been lost with the coming of double-ended cards. The Jack of Spades still faces to his left, but his halberd has long since been distorted to a strange curlicue without much meaning. The Jack of Clubs (sometimes in reverse position) still holds his pike, but his hat has acquired a small, decorative leaf, presumably derived from a feather on an earlier French pack.

This then, was the origin of the English pack, which has since spread throughout the world, and in particular, to the United States, which has adopted the pattern as its own. The first playing-cards to arrive on the American continent were undoubtedly Spanish, but the main source of American playing-cards in early times were the English and Dutch settlers. As early as 1633, records show that at Plymouth Colony several persons were fined £2 each for card-playing.

Despite the prohibitions, playing-cards continued to be imported from England, and this went on for some years after the American Revolution. In time, of course, native American card-makers appeared, first of whom was Jazaniah Ford, born in Milton, Massachusetts, in 1757. Ford placed an advertisement for his home-made playing-cards in the *Columbian Sentinel* in the year 1811, offering such delights as 'best Eagles, Harry 8ths, Merry Andrews, Highlanders and Refuse'.

We owe to the United States one additional card to the English pack, the Joker. A feature of the game of euchre, once popular in America, is to call the Jack of the trump suit, and the Jack of the suit with the same colour, the 'Bower'. There were thus two 'Bowers' in the game, until an extra card was introduced, and dubbed the Best Bower. This card was later renamed the Joker, and included in all new packs, spreading eventually to the United Kingdom, and indeed to the world.

Today, there is very little difference between packs made in the United Kingdom and in the United States. In fact, both countries import English-pattern packs made in almost every card-producing country in the world, which indicates that there is universal acceptance of the design.

ITALY

Packs of playing-cards using French suits are used in the north-west of Italy, that is, Piedmont, Liguria, Tuscany and Lombardy. There are five different patterns, all of which are still in use, including one which is shared with the neighbouring Swiss canton of Ticino, taken by the Swiss from Italy in 1512. The five patterns are:

Milanese or Lombard pattern (Milanesi telate)
This pack is used, as its name implies, in Lombardy and the Milan area, and also in the Italian-speaking areas of Switzerland. There are either 40 or 52 cards to a pack, almost always double-ended, and of the usual small Italian format, about 95mm × 50mm. As with other Italian French-suited packs, the cards have no indices.

All the Jacks bear some heraldic device, however small. The Jack of Hearts has a small badge on his chest, the Jack of Spades has a badge on his back, and the Jack of Diamonds is slipping off his coat to reveal a coat of arms on his back. The Jack of Clubs has a shield on his chest, with a device showing a human figure being devoured by a serpent. The King of Diamonds has a bird sitting on his arm, and the King of Spades wears a necklace, which hangs down his back.

Florentine pattern (Carte Fiorentine Grandi)
As their name suggests, these cards are larger than the normal Italian cards, about 65mm × 100mm. They are single-ended, and a pack usually contains 40 cards. Main characteristics are: The Kings of

46. Milanese pattern: King of Diamonds and Jack of Hearts

47. Florentine pattern: King of Hearts and Jack of Hearts

Diamonds and Hearts both possess scrolls on which the name of the maker is frequently shown, while the Jack of Clubs carries a large book, also inscribed with the maker's name. The Jack of Spades carries a shield, and the Jack of Hearts holds a large ornamental club.

Tuscan pattern (Carte Toscane)
This is a smaller variety of pack, which is similar to the Florentine, also consisting of 40 cards. These are about 90mm × 60mm in size. Packs vary to some extent, since some described as *carte Toscane* are merely smaller versions of the Florentine pattern. However, a variety of the pack exists in which the Queens wear no crowns, and the wearing apparel has a less 'rich' appearance. Special features of the design are: all Kings hold short sceptres or batons, Queens are crownless, while the Jack of Spades carries a short spear and the Jack of Hearts holds an arrow.

Genoese pattern (Genovesi telate)
The pack used in the Genoa area of Italy is almost identical with that of the standard pack used in Belgium, which is very close to the Paris pattern. The Italians normally omit the indices, but otherwise the cards look very like their Belgian counterparts. Some makers, such as Piatnik of Vienna, supply cards for both countries, which makes it

48. Tuscan pattern: Jack of Clubs and Jack of Diamonds

49. Genoese pattern: King of Clubs and Jack of Hearts

50. Piedmont pattern: King of Diamonds and Jack of Spades

difficult to distinguish the two. To complicate matters, Piatnik uses a French style for the firm's name on the Genoese pack, identifying the cards by an inscription on the label: *carte Francesi*. There are usually either 40 or 52 cards.

Piedmont pattern (Piemontesi telate)
Although of the smaller Italian size, this is really little more than an adaptation of the Genoese pattern. There are, however, some minor differences, the main one being that double-ended cards are divided not diagonally, as with the normal Paris pattern, but horizontally. Cards are about 82mm × 53mm, and are also found single-ended. All the Jacks carry halberds, and the King of Diamonds has a small sceptre in his hand.

SWITZERLAND

Ticinese pattern
This is identical to the Milanese or Lombard pattern (qv) as used in Northern Italy.

French-Swiss pattern
The Piquet pack used in Switzerland follows the Berliner pattern for the most part, although the design is much more restrained, and the court figures less flamboyantly attired. Such differences as exist are:

No shield appears on the King of Clubs card. The Queen of Clubs and the Queen of Diamonds have turned their heads from left to right. All the Jacks carry halberds, but the only Jack visibly holding the hilt of a sword is that of Clubs. Suitmarks appear in the blades of the halberds (cf the Russian standard pack). The Jack of Spades carries a shield. There are normally 36 cards to a pack, and these are slightly smaller than normal, about 57mm × 88mm.

51. Swiss Piquet: King of Clubs and Jack of Hearts

GERMANY

Although originally based on the Paris pattern, German cards using French suits have developed along their own lines, and can be classified into two distinctive types. Variations of both are used elsewhere, including the Scandinavian countries. The names given below have been adopted here for ease of reference, since German card manufacturers vary in their use of descriptive terms. In fact, both

German packs are commonly described as simply *Französisches Bild*, or French pattern.

Berliner, or *North-West German pattern (Berliner Bild)*
Normally found only with double-ended courts, this pack could be regarded as the standard French-suited pack for the whole of Germany, both East and West. It is produced by makers in all parts of

the country, and is available, according to the games for which it is to be used, in packs of 32, 36 or 52 cards. There are also packs containing two duplicate sets of 24 cards. Size of cards is about 60mm × 90mm.

The design is ornate, and the Jacks in particular are dressed in a rather flamboyant mediaeval style. All the Queens carry flowers, but none wears a crown. They are shown full-face, except the Queen of Spades, who looks to her right. Three of the Kings carry sceptres, the exception being the King of Hearts who carries a short sword upright in his left hand, and in his right he holds an orb. The King of Clubs holds a shield in his right hand, and the King of Spades has a lyre. Three Kings are shown full-face, the King of Diamonds being in profile and looking to his left.

All the Jacks wear large plumed hats, and hold halberds in their left hands. With the exception of the Jack of Diamonds (and sometimes the Jack of Hearts), the Jacks are shown holding the hilt of a sword in their right hands. Three Jacks are shown full-face, the Jack of Diamonds being in profile and looking to his left. Indices used are the usual German K, D and B, but the English K, Q and J are sometimes found.

Rhineland or Frankfurt pattern (Rheinisches Bild or Frankfurter Bild)

Rather less ornate than the Berliner pattern, this is used in all parts of Germany, although it appears to be less popular. Cards are about 64mm × 93mm in size, and usually double-ended.

Three of the Kings carry sceptres, the exception being the King of Hearts, who carries a sword. Three Kings carry orbs in their right hands, but the King of Spades fingers a locket hanging from a chain around his neck. The King of Hearts is the only one in profile, and he looks to his right. All Kings have heavy, curly beards.

Three of the Queens carry flowers, but the Queen of Clubs holds a fan in her left hand. All the Queens wear crowns, but the Queen of Diamonds is the only one seen in profile, looking to her right. The

52. Berliner pattern: King of Hearts and Queen of Spades

53. Rhineland pattern: King of Hearts and Queen of Spades

Queen of Spades is not quite full-face, but is turning to her left.

The Jacks of Clubs and Diamonds hold halberds in their left hands, while the Jack of Hearts holds a sword pointing down. Only the Jacks of Diamonds and Spades wear plumed hats. Three are full-faced, while the Jack of Diamonds is in profile, looking to his right.

This pack, originally a Dondorf design, is commonly used in Poland, sometimes with English indices, and sometimes with the Polish K, D and W.

AUSTRIA

Two varieties of French-suited packs are in use in Austria, as well as in the other areas of Europe which once formed part of the Austro-Hungarian Empire.

The best-produced versions are made by the firm of Ferdinand Piatnik, who formerly also made the packs in their branch factories at Budapest, Cracow

A

B

C

D

E

F

MINAKUCHI

G

H

J

and Prague. Today, the successors of Piatnik continue to make the packs, with varying standards of quality.

The Austrian pattern (*Österreichisches Bild*, sometimes called *Wiener Bild*, or Vienna pattern), is a modern version of a pack produced for export in the sixteenth century by makers in Lyons. Later, card-makers from Lyons emigrated to Switzerland and Austria, taking their designs with them.

The two varieties both have double-ended courts, and the principal difference between them is in the style of the crowns worn by the Kings. One pack has crowns so tall that the top is cut by the line bordering the card, while the other has Kings with more usual style of crowns, which are drawn well clear of the border.

Austrian large-crown pattern (pattern A)

These cards are found in packs with either 32 or 52 cards. They come in two sizes, usually about 63mm × 92mm or perhaps slightly larger, and about 70mm × 106mm.

The Kings are all full-face, the Kings of Hearts and Clubs looking to their left, and the other two looking to their right. The King of Hearts carries a scroll in his left hand, often inscribed with very tiny figures, while the other Kings carry sceptres. The King of Spades bears the maker's name on a sash, although this is frequently left blank.

Three Queens carry flowers, while the Queen of Clubs points to one embroidered on her dress. Two of the Queens (Hearts and Spades) wear crowns with flat, mortar-board-like fronts. These two Queens are shown full-face, while the other two are in profile, looking towards their right.

Two Jacks (Hearts and Clubs) hold batons while the other two have halberds. The Jack of Hearts holds the hilt of a sword in his right hand. On some packs, the Jack of Hearts's baton carries a pennant, either blank or with the name of the town of manufacture. Jacks are full-face, except that of Clubs, who looks to his right.

Some packs have no indices, while others bear the

54. Austrian large-crown pattern: King of Spades and Jack of Hearts

55. Austrian small-crown pattern: King of Spades and Jack of Hearts

German K, D and B. They are currently made in Austria, Italy and Czechoslovakia.

Austrian small-crown pattern (pattern B)

This version is distinguished by having Kings whose crowns are clear of the border frame-line. The crowns are more usual-looking, with leaf-clusters and red stones inset. All the Kings carry sceptres, while the King of Spades also has a sash bearing the name of the maker. Three of the Queens carry flowers – a basketful in the case of the Queen of Spades, while the Queen of Clubs holds a small mirror.

The Queens of Hearts and Spades, as with the large-crown pattern, wear crowns with square fronts. Three Jacks carry halberds, the Jack of Hearts holding a staff with a small pennant, which is sometimes blank, and sometimes showing the name of the manufacturing town.

The Kings are full-faced; the Kings of Hearts and Diamonds glancing to their left, and the others to their right. Three Queens are in profile, and the Queen of Spades almost so, and all look to their right. The Jacks are full-face except that of Clubs, who looks to his right.

Packs are currently made in Austria (often with English indices), Czechoslovakia and Poland, where the local indices of K, D and W are employed.

SCANDINAVIA

Cards with courts similar to both the Berliner and Rhineland patterns are in use in the Scandinavian countries, sometimes with rather more ornate designs. On the other hand, makers in Sweden, Denmark, Norway and Finland have produced packs which deviate widely from the standard packs used elsewhere, and also from each other.

The largest of the Scandinavian manufacturers is J. O. Öberg, of Eskilstuna, Sweden, who seems to have gone furthest in producing what could be regarded as a standard Swedish pack. Another type is used in Denmark, which follows fairly conventional lines, but cannot really be regarded as standard. Indices are K, D, Kn, and E (for Ace).

56. Scandinavian pattern: Sweden; King of Hearts and Queen of Clubs

57. Scandinavian pattern: Denmark; King of Hearts and Queen of Clubs

BELGIUM AND HOLLAND

The Low Countries have been producing cards for centuries, and a well-known reference to early card-making in the area is found in the account-book belonging to Johanna, Duchess of Brabant and her husband Wenceslaus of Luxembourg. The entry, which is dated 14 May 1379, reads: 'Given to Monsieur and Madame four peters, two florins, value eight and a half moutons, wherewith to buy a pack of cards.'

Today, varieties of the Paris pattern are commonly used in Belgium and Holland, each having reached a stage where it can be regarded as a standard Belgian, and a standard Dutch pack.

However, the Berliner, Rhineland and standard Paris patterns are also found. A popular practice in

PLATE 16
A. René Sturbelle pack by Van Genechten; B. 'Troubadour' by Catel & Farcy; C. 'Jeu des Têtes' by Création Pastor; D. 'Naipes Casino' by Justo Rodero e Hijos, Buenos Aires; E. Modernisation of the Spanish national pattern, by Fournier; F. 'Dauphins' by Catel & Farcy; G. 'Mizuno' by Nintendo; H. 'Fussball Skat' by F. X. Schmid for Fusska; J. 'Adidas' sporting pack by Grimaud.

RUGBY FOOTBALL

both countries is to include Aces with a different scenic picture at each end.

Belgian pattern

Belgian packs use the Paris pattern, without the names used in France. The execution of the design is usually rather more colourful on Belgian cards, which use the combination of black, green, yellow and red, rather than the black, blue, yellow and red common in France. Flemish indices of H, V and B are in use, as well as the French R, D and V, and there are the normal 52 cards to a pack, sometimes with additional jokers. An almost identical pattern, less indices, is used in the Genoa region of Italy.

Dutch pattern

The only remaining card-maker in Holland went out of business recently, so at present cards for the Dutch market are produced abroad, largely in Belgium. Cards with what might be regarded as the Dutch pattern are also found in Belgium and occasionally elsewhere, for instance in Scandinavia. It is somewhat similar to the Berliner pattern, with these main characteristics:

All Kings carry sceptres, including the King of Hearts. The crowns have a less 'regal' look than in the Berliner pattern. Only one Queen, that of Clubs, holds a flower. The Queen of Hearts has a small bird perching on her fingers, the Queen of Diamonds has a tiny mirror, and the Queen of Spades has what is probably a fan, although it could be a mirror. All the Queens have crowns.

The Jacks all carry halberds, with the Jack of Hearts holding the hilt of a sword, and not the Jack of Clubs as in the Berliner. The Jack of Spades also holds the hilt of a sword. The Kings are all full-face, as are the Jacks, but the Queen of Spades is seen in

58. Belgian pattern: King of Diamonds and Queen of Spades

59. Dutch pattern: King of Clubs and Jack of Hearts

profile, looking to her left. Normal Dutch indices are H, V and B (*Heer* = King; *Vrouw* = Queen; *Boer* = Jack). Occasionally packs using this pattern are found with Scandinavian indices.

PORTUGAL

At one time, packs employed Italo-Portuguese suit-marks, but nowadays the French suits prevail. The Portuguese standard pack is another variety of the Paris pattern, somewhat similar to the Berliner and Rhineland patterns. The King of Hearts carries a sceptre and orb, the Kings of Clubs and Diamonds both carry a sword and a shield, and the King of Spades carries a sword and an orb. Three Queens (Hearts, Clubs and Diamonds) carry flowers, while

the Queen of Diamonds also has a fan in her right hand. The Queen of Spades holds a folded fan. All Queens wear crowns. Three Jacks (Hearts, Diamonds and Spades) carry halberds, while the Jack of Clubs carries a spear in one hand and a shield in the other. The Jack of Spades also carries a shield, the Jack of Diamonds a sword, only the hilt of which is showing, and the Jack of Hearts has a hawk on his wrist.

USSR

Russian playing-cards date back to the end of the eighteenth century at least, using French suitmarks for the main part, although German suits are occasionally met with. Apart from the standard pack, about five other non-standard packs are currently available, some in small patience-sizes.

Standard pattern

The Russian pack is based on the Paris pattern, but is similar to the Berliner and Rhineland packs, and has several variations in the design. The King of Hearts is basically the same as that in the Rhineland pack, while the King of Clubs is based on his Berliner counterpart. The King of Diamonds wears a turban, and holds a sceptre ending in a crescent. He holds the hilt of a sword in his right hand, while the King of Spades resembles the Rhineland King, except that he is reversed and holds an orb as well as the sceptre.

All the Queens carry flowers and wear crowns. The Queen of Spades is in profile and looks to her right. All the Jacks carry halberds, each of which bears the suitmark on the blade, a feature also seen on Swiss piquet packs. Russian Jacks resemble those on the Berliner pattern, but the Jack of Hearts shows a shield, and the Jack of Clubs has a shield attached to his right arm. The Jack of Spades has his hand on the hilt of a sword. Russian indices are K, Д, В and Т (phonetically equivalent to K, D, V and T). Packs are made with and without frame-lines.

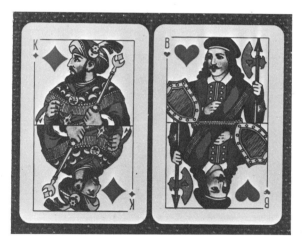

61. Russian standard pattern: King of Diamonds and Jack of Hearts

8
TAROT AND MINCHIATE CARDS

Tarot cards have been the subject of more discussion than any other known cards. Much has been written about them, particularly on their so-called occult aspect. They became connected with fortune-telling some time during the late eighteenth century, especially after the publication in 1781 of *Le Monde primitif* by the French scholar, Antoine Court de Gébelin (1725–84), son of a Protestant minister. The magical significance of Tarot cards, according to Court de Gébelin, was that they derived from the *Book of Thoth*, a mystical and mythical work supposed to have been written by the ancient Egyptian deity Thoth himself. By a study of this book, or of the Tarot cards which were said to have been based upon it, the reader could delve deep into occult matters.

A mass of pseudo-scientific literature followed, especially towards the latter half of the nineteenth century, when it coincided with the French 'occult' movement and the writings of such people as R. Falconnier in 1896, and 'Papus' (Gérard Encausse) in 1910.

In 1856 Eliphas Lévi (Alphonse-Louis Constant) claimed to have found a connection between the trumps of the Tarot pack and the Hebrew alphabet, each letter of which was believed by students of cabalistic matters to have a spiritual power.

In the years since these books were written, a host of others have followed, and the 'science' of Tarot card reading has developed to such a degree that all manner of mystic powers have been ascribed to them. Packs have been eagerly seized upon by a variety of fortune-tellers, soothsayers and astrologers.

Tarot cards existed, of course, well before the eighteenth century. In fact, Tarots are among the earliest known playing-cards, but there seems to be very little evidence prior to Court de Gébelin's writings in 1781 to suggest that anyone believed them to possess any more mystique than other packs of cards. Playing-cards of all kinds have been used for fortune-telling, particularly by such people as the gypsies, but Tarots were only mysterious because they were unfamiliar.

Like other playing-cards, Tarots were, and still are, used for playing a game. They originated in Italy, and spread to other countries to the north, such as Austria, Hungary, southern France and Switzerland. Just when this spread took place is unknown, but for some reason they rarely went farther north. It seems likely, however, that an odd pack or two would have been carried by travellers. Among the best-known of the European travellers,

COLOUR PLATE 5

A. The King of Clubs from an historical pack made c1920 in Austria for sale in Scandinavia.
B. The Queen of Clubs from a German pack made to commemorate the Frankfurt Schützfest (shooting festival) of 1862.
C. The King of Diamonds from a pack made by Dondorf for the Boer War. This card depicts M. T. Stein, president of the Orange Free State.
D. The Queen of Diamonds from an advertising pack made for Lyons teashops c1930 by De La Rue.
E. The Queen of Clubs from a pack made for Bulgaria c1950 by De La Rue.
F. The King of Hearts from a pack made c1880 by Reynolds and Sons, England.
G. The Unter of Sunflowers (equivalent to the Bells suit) from a pack made c1893 by Dr Schroeter of Jena, Germany. This pack has recently been reprinted.
H. A very early pack made c1650 by Pierre Barbey, of France. This card, which is the Seven of Animals, also bears the Spades suitmark.
J. The King of Spades from a standard English pack made by De La Rue c1880.

A

B

C

D

E

F

G

H

J

A

B

C

D

Queen Charlotte of England
A Moral lady
with fifteen children

E

F

G

H

J

of course, were the gypsies, and since they were fond of using cards for divination, it seems probable that they brought examples of Tarot cards from Italy.

To the uninitiated, a traditional Tarot pack, with its archaic designs, would look very odd indeed; small wonder therefore that special qualities began to be ascribed to them.

The composition of a full Tarot pack, which has 78 cards, falls into two groups:

(a) Fifty-six cards divided into the 4 Italian suits of Coins, Cups, Swords and Batons. Each suit has 14 cards, including 4 court-cards: King, Queen, Knight and Jack; and 10 numerical cards from Ten to Ace.

(b) The second group consists of 22 special trump cards, which bear no suitmarks, but are numbered from 21 to 1, the last card, or Fool, being unnumbered. Each trump card bears a picture, the design of which is thought to have originated during the fifteenth century.

It seems unlikely that the designs used on the trumps of the Tarot pack were the only ones known, or that they were devised without any plan or over-all pattern. What does seem likely is that the trump designs were devised separately, perhaps with some religious motive.

In all probability the standard part of the pack was already in use separately, the final Tarot pack of 78 cards coming into being as the result of an amalgamation of the standard, suited pack with one of the existing pictorial packs.

The origin of the word 'Tarot' itself has been the subject of some discussion, as yet unresolved. The Italians called it *tarocco*, although even this name was not used until the early sixteenth century. Before that date, the game was referred to as Triumphs (*trionfi*), which is an earlier form of the word *trump*. Other languages use variations of the Italian form, but etymological evidence is lacking.

ITALIAN-SUITED TAROTS

Today, varieties of the Italian-suited Tarots survive in Italy, France and Switzerland. Although originating in Italy, Tarot cards usually have their names shown in French, though other packs exist with Italian or even English titles. The 22 trumps are listed on p 73.

Italian-suited packs presently in use are as follows:

Tarot de Marseille
As the name suggests, this is the usual Tarot pack to be found in France. It follows the usual Tarot style and design, with 78 cards, about 123mm × 65mm in size. Early versions and modern copies of them frequently mis-spell the French, while the title of the

COLOUR PLATE 6
A. The 'Hunting Skat' pack from Germany, which shows game animals on all the court-cards and Aces. Hunting symbols have been superimposed on the suitmarks.
B. A 'mediaeval' style pack with unusually-designed suitmarks, issued in Belgium c1940.
C. The 'Wagner' pack, made in Switzerland, and featuring the composer's operas. Designed in 1920, it was not printed until 1968.
D. The Royal Dynasty pack, made in Belgium in 1934. Various members of the Belgian Royal family are shown, the Queen of Hearts depicting Queen Astrid.
E. 'Grand Slam', a double pack made in England in 1970 for the 200th anniversary of the Battle of Trenton New Jersey, 1776. One pack shows British leaders and the other, American.
F. The Queen of Diamonds shown here represents Maria Theresia, from an Austrian pack called 'Madame Pompadour'.
G. The King of Hearts shown here is Napoleon, from a pack made in France for the bicentenary of the Emperor's birth in 1969.
H. The King of Hearts here represents Solomon, from an Israeli pack depicting Biblical characters.
J. The King of Spades in this pack shows a Sassanian sovereign, while other courts have various Iranian rulers. Made in Spain.

A

B

a bad
trip is no
picnic

C

D

E

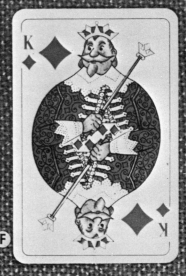

F

© WALT DISNEY PRODUCTIONS

G

H

J

No	Italian	French	English
I	Il Bagattel Il Bagatto	Le Bateleur	The Juggler or Mountebank
2*	La Papessa	La Papesse	The Female Pope or High Priestess
3	L'Imperatrice	L'Impératrice	The Empress
4	L'Imperatore	L'Empereur	The Emperor
5*	Il Papa	Le Pape	The Pope
6	Gli Amanti	L'Amoureux	The Lovers or Marriage
7	Il Carro	Le Chariot	The Chariot
8	La Giustizia	La Justice	Justice
9	L'Eremita	L'Hermite or Le Vieillard	The Hermit or The Old Man
10	Rota di Fortune Ruota della Fortuna	La Roue de Fortune	Wheel of Fortune
11	La Forza	La Force	Fortitude Strength Force
12	Il Penduto Lo Impiccato L'Appéso	Le Pendu	The Hanging Man The Hanged Man
13†	La Morte	—	Death
14	La Temperanza	Tempérance	Temperance
15	Il Diavolo	Le Diable	The Devil
16	La Torre	La Maison Dieu	The Tower
17	Le Stelle	L'Etoile	The Star or Stars
18	La Luna	La Lune	The Moon
19	Il Sole	Le Soleil	The Sun
20	Il Giudizio L'Angelo	Le Jugement	Judgement
21	Il Mondo	Le Monde	The World
22 or 0	Il Matto	Le Mat Le Fol	The Fool

* In the 1800 Besançon pack, and present-day Swiss packs, No 2 becomes Juno, and No 5 becomes Jupiter. Compare, too, the Belgian Tarot pack dating from the eighteenth century, in which Trump No II is called *Capitano Eracasse-Lespagnol* and Trump No V shows *Bacus* (Bacchus).

† Unnamed on French packs, and on some others.

PLATE 17
A. 'Essberger' pack by F. X. Schmid; B. 'Michelin' pack by Grimaud; C. 'Trip-trap' anti-drug pack by Stancraft Products, Minneapolis; D. 'Harlequin' pack for Tiffany, reprinted by US Playing Card Co; E. 'Loriot' skat pack by ASS; F. 'Four Centuries' by Öberg; G. Walt Disney pack by Plastic Cards, Milan; H. 'Happy Playing Cards' by F. X. Schmid; J. Apothecary pack by Müller for Dr E. Brum-Antonioli.

pack, when shown, is often prefixed by the words *Grand* or *Ancien*.

In some early packs, the names of *Le Pape* and *La Papessa* had been expunged and *Le Grandprêtre* and *La Grandprêtresse* (The High Priest and the High Priestess) substituted, while a pack from Besançon dated 1800 changed the names to Jupiter and Juno. Other variations included altering trump No XII from *Le Pendu* to *La Prudence*, Nos III and IV from *L'Impératrice* and *L'Empereur* to *La Grand Mère* and *Le Grand Père*, and No II to *Le Printemps*.

Apart from the trumps, there are the 56 standard cards as described above, with 4 court-cards and Ace and 9 numerical cards to each suit. Trumps are numbered with either Arabic or Roman numerals.

Swiss version

A variety of Italian-suited Tarots is made in Switzerland by J. Müller & Cie, of Schaffhausen. There are the usual 78 cards, size 111mm × 61mm. The design follows an eighteenth-century, or early nineteenth-century pattern rather than the traditional style of the *Ancien Tarot*. Like the Besançon pack of 1800, trumps No II and V are Juno and Jupiter. The court-cards are single-ended. Other, earlier, Swiss packs are similar to those used in France and Italy.

Piedmont Tarot (*Tarocco Piemontese*)

This follows the traditional Tarot pattern, having 78 cards made up of 22 trumps and 4 suits of 14 cards each. Both trumps and court-cards are usually double-ended, and the trumps are numbered with Arabic figures, except for No 22 – The Fool – which is unnumbered and bears no name.

Earlier versions, which had 'turnover' edges, a feature of old Italian cards, were single-ended and were numbered with Roman numerals. The size of the cards is usually about 107mm × 64mm. The style of the design follows that of such Italian packs as the Venetian and Piacentine patterns, while the trump cards use the conventional names, shown in Italian.

Bologna Tarot (*Tarocco Bolognese*)

A rather more distinctive pack comes from the district around Bologna in Italy. Containing only 62 cards, and known therefore as a *tarocchino* or 'little Tarot', the Bologna pack suppresses Twos,

62. Tarot de Marseille: King of Batons and La Papesse (the Female Pope)

63. Tarot, Swiss version: King of Batons and Trump No 2, Juno

PLATE 18
A and B. Dondorf pack No 133 with pictorial Aces. Other pictorial Aces from: C. A pack by Speelkaarten Nederland; D. A Dondorf Rhineland pattern pack; E and F. A pair of packs by VSS Altenburg; G. A Belgian pack with Rhineland-type courts; H. A German-made pack with English-pattern courts; J. A Belgian-type pack made in Hungary.

A

B

C

D

E

F

G

H

J

64. Piedmont Tarot: King of Batons and the Female Pope

65. Bologna Tarot: King of Batons and the Angel

Threes, Fours and Fives of each suit. Thus there are only 10 cards to a suit instead of 14. There are, however, 22 trumps, of which Nos 5–16 are given numbers, shown in Arabic numerals, the rest being blank.

All trumps are unnamed, the subjects being: the Juggler, 4 cards with figures which appear as Moors in earlier packs (2 identical in appearance), but which are now shown as somewhat effeminate Europeans carrying spears, the Moon, the Sun, the Angel, the World, and the Fool. All these are without numbers,

the remainder, with their numbers, being:

No 5, the Lovers; No 6, the Chariot; No 7, Temperance; No 8, Justice; No 9, Fortitude; No 10, the Wheel of Fortune; No 11, the Hermit; No 12, the Hanging Man; No 13, Death; No 14, the Devil; No 15, the Tower; and No 16, the Star.

The cards are double-ended, both court-cards and trumps, and measure about 108mm × 53mm. A version of this pack, minus the trumps and the 4 Queens is sold *es* the *Bologna Pattern*. At one time, the design showed single-figured courts.

Sicilian Tarot (*Tarocco Siciliano*)

Since this pack contains only 64 cards, it is a 'little Tarot' or *tarocchino*. It is the only Tarot to use Italo-Portuguese suitmarks, and follows the style, though not the design, of the Sicilian regional pattern. The cards are small in size, about 80mm × 50mm, in keeping with the regional cards of the area. They are single-ended, and packs contain the usual 4 court-cards in each suit. The Jacks, however, are female, and each has a shield. Kings also have shields. Aces, Twos, Threes, Fours are suppressed, so that numerical cards run from Five up to Ten, although an extra Ace of Coins is included.

None of the trumps is named, but 20 are numbered, while the Pope, Female Pope and the Devil have been suppressed in favour of a female figure, a ship and a beggar. The trumps of the Sicilian Tarot are, therefore:

1, the Juggler; 2, the Empress; 3, the Emperor; 4, Fortitude; 5, Temperance; 6, a female figure (Constancy); 7, Justice; 8, The Lovers; 9, The Chariot; 10, The Wheels of Fortune; 11, the

PLATE 19
Patience and miniature packs: A. Dondorf; B. 'Luxury No 26' by Piatnik; C. Rococo style by Müller; D. 'Pattern No 119' by Piatnik; E. Czechoslovak pack by Casino; F. Miniature piquet pack by Müller; G. Miniature Jass pack by Müller; H. Čedok Interhotel pack by Casino, Prague; J. Rococo pack by F. X. Schmid; K. 'Gold Lady' pack by ASS; L. 'Dandy' confectionery pack 'Our Modern Army'; M. 'Bluebird' African Safari pack by Nintendo; N. Special design used on matchbox labels for a Dutch supermarket, designed by Han Janssen; O. Mini-patience by F. X. Schmid; P. 'Confidenze', a pop-style pack from Italy; Q. 'Grotesque', by Vito Arienti; R. 'Sweetule' Natural History pack; S. A pack from Belgium by Brépols.

A

B

C

D

E

F

G

H

J

K

L

M

N

O

P

Q

R

S

66. Sicilian Tarot: King of Batons and Trump No 14, the Ship

67. Minchiate cards: Knight of Coins and Trump No 26, the Scorpion

but with the addition of cards presenting the twelve signs of the Zodiac, four Virtues, and four Elements. The first 35 cards are numbered with Roman numerals, the last 6 remaining unnumbered.

No titles are shown on the trumps, which for convenience here are given English titles as follows:

I	The Mountebank	XXI	Water
II	The Grand Duke	XXII	Earth
III	The Western Emperor	XXIII	Air
		XXIIII	The Scales
IIII	The Eastern Emperor	XXV	The Virgin
		XXVI	The Scorpion
V	The Lovers	XXVII	The Ram
VI	Temperance	XXVIII	The Goat
VII	Fortitude	XXVIIII	The Archer
VIII	Justice	XXX	The Crab
VIIII	The Wheel of Fortune	XXXI	The Fishes
		XXXII	The Water-Carrier
X	The Chariot		
XI	The Hermit	XXXIII	The Lion
XII	The Hanging Man	XXXIIII	The Bull
		XXXV	The Twins
XIII	Death		
XIIII	The Devil	*Unnumbered:*	
XV	The Tower		The Star
XVI	Hope		The Moon
XVII	Prudence		The Sun
XVIII	Faith		The Angel
XVIIII	Charity		The World
XX	Fire		The Fool

Minchiate packs sometimes have a somewhat crude appearance, but the designs are quite distinctive, particularly on the court-cards. The Knights are shown as half-human, half-animal, with, for instance, the Knight of Swords appearing as a Centaur, and Knight of Coins as a man with the hindquarters of a lion. Two of the Jacks (Swords and Batons) are male, as usual, but those of Cups and Coins are female.

Except for the court-cards, the Swords used in the suit of that name are straight, unlike the curved style normally used on Italian cards (see Addenda, p 112). Small vignetted drawings of various animals appear on the numerical cards of each suit.

The rest of the pack is made up of the 4 standard suits of 14 cards: King, Queen, Knight, Jack, Ace, and numerical cards from 10–2.

Hanged Man (actually portrayed as hanging by the neck, instead of by the feet as in other Tarots); 12, the Hermit; 13, Death; 14, the Ship; 15, the Tower; 16, the Star; 17, the Moon; 18, the Sun; 19, the World; 20, Judgement; and the last two, which are unnumbered, are the Beggar and the Fool.

Minchiate packs

Florentine Tarot packs with 41 trumps are called *Minchiate* packs, having a total of 97 cards. Although no longer made, having last been in use during the end of the last century, *Minchiate* packs are still occasionally met with. The trumps are made up of some of the usual 22 trumps from the normal Tarot,

9
FRENCH-SUITED TAROTS AND FORTUNE-TELLING CARDS

About the middle eighteenth century, another variety of Tarot cards made their appearance, with French suitmarks instead of the traditional Italian. At first, the packs contained the usual 78 cards, but these gradually gave way to a 54-card pack, in which 24 cards were omitted. These are the Five to Ten in the red suits, and the Ace to Six in the black suits. Such packs are still made in Germany, Austria, Hungary, Czechoslovakia, Switzerland, France, and, until recently, Italy.

The design and execution is quite different from the Italian-suited packs, although there remain 4 suits, each with 4 court-cards, plus 22 trumps. The court-cards of most packs are very similar, and seem to have originated in southern Germany, sometime in the eighteenth century. There are, however, some early packs known which were issued minus the trumps and Knights, and which could be regarded as another German regional pattern with French suitmarks. It may be, therefore, that the French-suited Tarot packs were based on a regional pattern which has now ceased to exist.

GERMANY

French-suited Tarot packs now made in Germany are called Cego cards, and are made for a game of that name. There are two basic patterns:

Standard Cego pattern
Originally, this contained 78 cards, but the present-day Cego packs consist of 54 cards, about 112mm × 63mm in size. Court-cards are King, Queen, Knight and Jack in each suit, together with numerical cards as detailed above. All modern cards are double-ended, including the trumps, which are numbered from 1 to 21 in Arabic numerals, while the Fool, following the style of the court-cards, is unnumbered.

The trumps show country people at work and play; each card has two pictures, depicting 'work' at one end, and 'play' at the other. The maker's name is usually shown on the Ace of Hearts.

Adler Cego pattern
Despite its name, no Eagle appears on these cards, the courts of which are different from those of the standard Cego. Again, there are 54 cards of about the same size, the pack being constituted in the same way as before. The design of the courts is somewhat reminiscent of the Berliner pattern, but there are major differences. The Queens all carry flowers, all the Jacks hold halberds, and two of the Knights (Clubs and Hearts) appear in armour.

Both the King and Knight of Diamonds wear a

68 Standard German Cego: King of Spades and Trump No 10

kind of Turkish costume, and the Fool, as in the standard Cego, plays a guitar. The trumps are numbered in Arabic figures from 21 to 1, and are double-ended, as are the courts. Pictures are different at each end of the trump cards, and all (with the exception of No 1, which shows a stage musician) illustrate various animals, including a very odd-looking lion minus his hindquarters on trump No 2. The Adler Cego is now sold as standard, but earlier Cego packs with animal themes were single-ended, and bore Roman numerals on the trumps.

AUSTRIA AND HUNGARY

As in Germany, there have been a variety of French-suited Tarot packs, but at the present time, only one is made, with two minor varieties.

Standard Tarot pattern

This is sometimes referred to as the *Industrie und Glück* (Industry and Good Fortune) Tarot, since these words are shown prominently on trump No II. The pattern appears to have first been issued about the year 1830, and the present versions indicate a nineteenth-century origin. The cards are about 115mm × 63mm in size, and are double-ended. There are 54 cards to a pack, each of the 4 suits consisting of King, Queen, Knight, Jack and 4 numerical cards. Hearts and Diamonds have Ace to Four, and Spades and Clubs have Seven to Ten. There are 22 trumps, numbered in Roman numerals from XXI to I, the Fool being unnumbered.

The pattern of the courts is similar to that adopted by the German Cego packs, but the style is much more ornate, and the modern packs show a remarkable amount of detail. The maker's name is usually shown on the Jacks of Clubs and Diamonds, and also on the Ace of Hearts.

Each of the trumps carries two pictures illustrating scenes from the folklore of the countries which belonged to the Austro-Hungarian Empire. The figures shown include peasants at work and play, lovers, sailors, eastern potentates and even Scotsmen.

The two varieties of this pack can be recognised by the different pictures which appear on the trump

70. Austrian standard Tarot: Style A. King of Spades and Trump No 1

cards, and a minor variation in the style of the court-cards. For reference, these are here distinguished as:

Style A: Trump No 1 shows a girl dancing with a tambourine, while the other end of the card has a young man in costume playing a dulcimer or zither.

Style B: Trump No 1 shows the dancing girl with tambourine as before, but the young man plays, not a zither, but a harp. Trump No 2 is the same in each case, but the pictures shown on the rest of the trumps are either different in each style, or appear on different trump cards.

Ferdinand Piatnik of Vienna makes packs in both Style A and Style B, and a version of Style A is also made in Czechoslovakia, and before World War II, was made in Germany. Style B was also made until recently in Hungary, and not long ago, Modiano of Trieste was making a pack which was a combination of both. Outside the German-speaking countries, the words *Industrie und Glück* is omitted from trump No 2, and in Hungary, is replaced by *Szerencse Fel!* A smaller version of Style B is also made by the Hungarian card-making enterprise, size 100mm × 60mm. (See also note on p 112.)

FRANCE AND SWITZERLAND

72. French and Swiss pattern Tarot: King of Spades (Swiss) and Trump No 1 (French)

Except for some minor variations in the pictures shown on the trump cards, the packs made in these two countries are practically the same. There are 78 cards to a pack, size about 112mm × 60mm, which are double-ended, and consist of the full 4 suits (King, Queen, Knight, Jack and Ten to Ace). There are 22 trumps, including the Fool, which is unnumbered. Court-cards resemble the German Cego pack closely, and as in that version, have the Fool playing a guitar.

The trumps are numbered in Arabic numerals from 21 to 1. As with other French-suited Tarot packs, two pictures are shown on each trump card, the scenes being nineteenth-century, and showing people at work and play, including such activities as shopping, fishing, dancing, skating, card-playing etc. French cards usually have the monogram of the maker on the corner of each trump card.

OTHER TAROTS

With the rise of interest in Tarot cards, particularly the Italian-suited ones, new designs have appeared, and are still appearing. Among the better-known examples is the French-suited Ditha Moser pack, made in 1906 by Berger of Vienna, and designed by Frau Ditha Moser. This 54-card pack, made in the *Jugendstil* manner, was printed in a limited edition of only one hundred packs, although a reprint was made recently.

Another, using Italian suits, was the Waite Tarot,

a 78-card pack, designed by Pamela Coleman Smith to the order of A. E. Waite, originally issued in the United States in 1911, and reprinted subsequently. Produced to satisfy the demand for an 'occult' pack, suits were named on the cards as Cups, Wands (Batons), Swords and Pentacles (Coins). Jacks were shown as pages, and there were the usual 22 trumps, the whole pack being drawn in the *art nouveau* style.

There has even been a 'pop' Tarot, in which the 22 trumps include such innovations as a picture of

A — CRISTÓBAL COLÓN
Descubridor de América, 1492

B — Navarra

C

D — Sagrada Familia - BARCELONA

E — 金閣寺 Kinkaku-ji Temple

F — CORBACHO - 1963

G — THE VIEUX CARRE, NEW ORLEANS

H — CITY HALL, TORONTO

J — THE CATHEDRAL, CHRISTCHURCH

the Chariot as a young woman riding a motor-cycle. This was produced in the USA, as were such offerings as an 'Egyptian' Tarot made by the 'Church of Light', and an Aquarian Tarot for the 'Age of Aquarius'. In 1973 the film *Live and Let Die* showed James Bond using a special pack of Tarot cards to decide his fate, and later the cards were issued commercially. The pack was designed by a Scottish artist, Fergus Hall.

FORTUNE-TELLING CARDS

Although not strictly speaking playing-cards, fortune-telling packs have usually been derived, if somewhat haphazardly, from either standard playing-cards or from Tarot packs. Cards of all kinds have been, and still are, used for fortune-telling, but the special packs which have been made within the last 150 years are not without interest.

Court de Gébelin's writings led another Frenchman, Alliette, a wig-maker and fortune-teller, to produce a book of his own. Alliette used an anagram of his name – Etteilla – and proceeded to make it even better known by inventing his own Tarot pack, which he claimed was an 'authentic Egyptian' Tarot, with the 'mistakes corrected'.

Other writers came thick and fast, each claiming that Etteilla was wrong, and each seeking to show how the Tarot cards were secretly linked to ancient mysteries. Ideas led on to specially designed fortune-telling packs, quite remote from the original Tarots. Throughout the nineteenth century, such packs increased in number and popularity, many surviving to the present day, particularly in France, Italy and Germany.

Probably the best-known of the fortune-tellers producing their own brand of cards, complete with weird signs, symbols and antique-looking designs was Mlle Lenormand, whose fame spread far and wide, even to the Royal court of the Emperor Napoleon himself. She made a fortune for herself from her activities, and her name is still used to describe certain packs of fortune-telling cards.

73. Fortune-telling cards: Petit Cartomancien (France) and La Vera Sibilla (Italy)

74. Fortune-telling cards: two packs from Czechoslovakia

10
INDIAN AND PERSIAN PLAYING-CARDS

The generic name for playing-cards in India is *Ganjifa*. These are, for the most part, circular in shape, varying in size from 25mm to 100mm in diameter. Always hand-made, packs are produced from a variety of materials, such as thin wood, woven cotton fibre, paper, ivory, animal skins, leather or even fish-scales. The cards are painted in colours and finished with lacquer, which results in substantially bulky discs.

Playing-cards were known in India as long ago as the sixteenth century, and apart from a few packs influenced by the Portuguese, and at a later date by other Europeans, appear to be indigenous to the country. The earliest reference we have to them is found in the writings of the first Mogul emperor Baber (Fehir-ed-din-Mohammed), telling how he sent a pack of Ganjifa to Sind in 1527. Subsequently, in 1590, we learn of the claim of Akbar the Great (Jelal-ed-din-Mohammed) to have invented the 8-suited Ganjifa pack. The emperor knew also of an earlier pack containing 12 suits.

Indian playing-cards can be divided into six main groups:

1 Dasavatara (two types)
2 Ganjappa
3 Chad (thirteen types)
4 Ganjifa proper (three main types)
5 Military packs
6 European-type packs (three main types)

Individual packs under these headings are:

1 Dasavatara

The meaning of this word is 'ten incarnations', since the packs are devised and based on the ten incarnations of the Hindu deity Vishnu.

Type A (Savantvadi): This pack contains 120 cards divided into 10 suits, each representing an incarnation of the deity. There are 12 cards to a suit, 10 of

75. Indian cards: Dasavatara type: (*left*) Avatar of Conch suit; and (*right*) Pradhan of Water Vase suit

which are numerical cards indicated by suitmarks from One to Ten, and 2 court-cards. The first is *Avatara*, the manifestation of Vishnu himself, showing the deity in action or on a throne, and *Pradhan*, showing the deity either mounted on a horse or seated on a stool.

Suitmarks are: *Matsya* (the Fish); *Kurma* (the Tortoise); *Varaha* (the Wild Boar); *Narsimha* (the Lion); *Vamana* (the Dwarf); *Parasurama* (the Axe); *Rama* (the Bow and Arrow); *Krishna* (the Cow); *Buddha* (the Conch); and *Kalki* (the Horse). Suitmarks are sometimes replaced by other symbols, as: the Lion, by the Quoit; the Water Vase, by the Umbrella; the Bow and Arrow, by the Monkey; the Cow, by the Quoit, Plough or Club; the Conch,

76. Indian cards: Ganjappa type: (*left*) Ravana of Clubs suit; and (*right*) Rama of Arrows suit

by the Lotus; and the Horse, by the Sword. Suit-marks are repeated according to the value of the card.

Type B: There is a total of 384 cards in this pack, of which only one example is known. There are 22 suits or Avatars showing the incarnations of Vishnu, a further 8 suits of *Dikpalas*, or Guardians, and 2 extra suits, all with 10 numerical cards and 2 court-cards each. Court-cards are represented by a Divinity and a *Pradhan*.

2 Ganjappa

This is the Rama pack of Orissa, and contains 12 suits of 12 cards, making a total of 144 to a pack. Based on the military exploits in the Sanskrit epic *Ramayana*, the pack is divided into two groups of 6 suits. The first, known as the 'weak' suits, follows the prince Rama, and the other, or 'strong' suits, belong to Ravana, the giant of Ceylon.

The 2 court-cards in the first 6 suits are Rama and his Vizier (*Mantri*), and the second 6 suits have courts representing Ravana and his Vizier. Each suit has 10 numerical cards, with suitmarks as follows:

Rama suits: the Arrow, the Quiver, the Monkey, the Bear, the Hill and the Shield and Sword. *Ravana suits:* the Club, the Spear, the Noose or Snake, the Pica (tail-less hare), and the Sword. Some Ganjappa packs use suits similar to those found in Dasavatara packs, but with the addition of two more suits.

3 Chad

Packs grouped under this heading were apparently invented, for the most part, by Krishnaraja Wadiyar, ruler of Mysore. He was deposed in 1831, and hav-

ing some time on his hands for the next thirty years or so, spent them in devising various games. He also wrote a book, *The Treasure Book of Sports and Pastimes,* in which he describes thirteen different types of Chad packs.

Based on religious or astrological ideas, Chad packs vary in content from 36 cards to as many as 360, the number of suits ranging from 4 to 18. Most Chad packs have 6 court-cards founded on military precedence, showing elephants, chariots, horses, warriors and fortresses. Some packs contain extra 'trump' cards on the lines of Tarot packs, together with wild or 'joker' cards depicting various birds. Numerical cards sometimes use the signs of the Zodiac, together with the suitmark value.

The usual 6 Chad court-cards are: *Nayak*, or Presiding Deity; *Shakti*, or Consort; *Rath*, or Chariot; *Mantri*, or Horseman; *Yoddha*, or Warrior; and *Dhwaj*, or Banner on Fortress.

The Indian versions of the signs of the Zodiac, as shown on some Chad packs, are: *Mesha*, Aries;

COLOUR PLATE 7

A. The Deuce of Leaves from a special pack using a modern version of the Hungarian pattern. Made by the Hungarian playing-card enterprise for their 150th anniversary in 1969.

B. The Queen of Spades from the Russian jubilee pack issued in 1967 marking the 150th anniversary of Russian card-making.

C. Made in 1971 by Grimaud, this 'Genie', or King of Diamonds, is from a pack reproducing the 'Year Two' revolutionary pack of France, dating from the eighteenth century.

D. 'Rosier', a non-standard modern circular pack, made in Japan by Nintendo. The suits each have a different colour.

E. Another circular pack, showing the King of Clubs. It advertises the Scaldia paper firm, and was made in Belgium.

F. The King of Diamonds, depicting the statesman David Lloyd George. This combination playing-card and domino pack was issued with cigarettes in 1929.

G. 'Le Grand Jeu de Collection', a modern pack designed by Création Pastor, and issued in France in 1971.

H. 'Corsairs and Filibusters', featuring piratical characters, made in 1968 by G. Delluc in France.

J. 'Le Jeu de Blocus', issued in France in twin packs of 32 cards to commemorate the Napoleonic wars. One pack has characters from the French side, and the other depicts the Allies.

A

B

C

D

E

F

G

H

J

Vrishaba, Taurus; *Mithuna*, Gemini; *Karaka*, Cancer; *Simha*, Leo; *Kanya*, Virgo; *Tula*, Libra; *Vrischika*, Scorpio; *Dhanus*, Sagittarius; *Makara*, Capricorn; *Kumbha*, Aquarius; and *Meena*, Pisces.

The following table shows the content of the thirteen Chad packs described by Krishnaraja Wadiyar:

	Name of Chad	No of suits	Cards in suit		Extra cards		Total cards in pack
			Courts	Numerical	Trumps	Jokers	
1	Chamundeshvari	16	6	12*	25	7	320
2	Jagad Mohan	18	6	12	27	9	360
3	Navin Dasavatara (a)	14	5–6	7–12	21	5	242
	„ „ (b)	12	6	12	17	7	240
4	Naw Grah	12	6	12*	—	—	216
5	Panch Pandava	12	6	12	—	—	216
6	Devi Dasavatara	10		18	—	—	180
7	Dikpala	10		16	—	—	160
8	Manohar	9		16	9	7	160
9	Sarva Mangala	8		18	16	—	160
10	Nav Ratna	9		16	9	7	160
11	Sadje Jyatadi	6		12	—	—	72
12	Krishnaraja	4	5	13	—	—	72
13	Navin Rama	4	3	6	—	—	36

* Zodiac suits.

COLOUR PLATE 8

A. The Ten of Batons from a humorous pack made in Spain in 1967. Designed by the artist Mingote for the firm of Myr.

B. The Jack of Hearts from a similar humorous pack designed for Myr in 1968 by Mingote, this time with French suitmarks.

C. The Queen of Clubs from a humorous pack made for a Dutch marine-paint company. The courts are seamen and passengers.

D. This pack, called 'Kennedy Kards', was made in 1963 and has humorous courts showing members of the Kennedy family.

E. Another American pack called 'Politicards', each card showing a caricature of a politician. Ex-Vice-President Agnew is shown on the Jack of Spades.

F. Designed in 1964 by Bruzon, this 'Don Quixote' pack, made in Spain, shows humorous drawings of Don Quixote and Sancho Panza.

G. The King of Hearts from a publicity pack made in Belgium and sponsored by the State Mining Industry.

H. A humorous pack made in France to advertise a plumbing company, with court-cards showing engineers, plumbers and housewives.

J. A publicity pack made in Germany to advertise a brewing company. The courts show beer-drinkers.

4 Ganjifa Proper

Although the word *Ganjifa* is used in India to describe all playing-cards, it is also used for a specific type of pack, referred to here as Ganjifa Proper.

The Mogul Emperor Akbar the Great, according to his chronicler, Abul Fazl Allami, was familiar with both four-sided, and two-sided chess, as well as with an old card game containing 12 suits. Finding this game too clumsy, the Emperor devised the eight-suited game of Ganjifa, of which three types are now known:

(a) *Akbar's Game:* This is a pack containing 96 cards divided into 8 suits of 12. There are 2 court-cards, *Mir* and *Vizier*, which can be roughly approximated to 'Chief of State' or 'King', and 'Prime Minister'. There are 10 numerical cards.

Suits are divided into 'weak' and 'strong'; and represent divisions of the Imperial Court:

Weak suits: *Surukh*, or Gold suit, representing the Treasury, with suitmarks of gold discs; *Bharat*, for the Chancellery (small oblongs); *Quimash*, for the Stores (divided ovals); and *Chang*, representing Royal Music (lyres).

Strong suits: *Safet*, representing the Silver Mint

F

77. Indian cards: (*left to right*) Six of Spades from Piquet pack; Fish (Matsya) of Vishnu suit from Krishnaraja Chad; and One of Soldier suit from Military-type pack

78. Indian cards: Ganjifa type: (*left*) Mir of Gholam suit; and (*right*) Mir of Surukh suit

(white discs, or Moons); *Shamsher*, for the Sword and Armoury (swords); *Taj*, for the Crown and Royal Insignia (crowns); and *Gholam*, for the Servants of the Household (men and women).

Distinctive features of the pack are to be noted in the *Surukh* suit, in which the Mir is shown as the Sun riding a lion, while the Mir of *Gholam* rides an elephant. The Vizier of *Gholam* rides a bullock, while that of the *Chang* suit (usually shown as a woman) rides a camel.

(b) *Orissa Type:* Variations of this pack made in Orissa show quite different suitmarks, with the Mir altered to Rama, and the Vizier becoming Lakshman, Virupaksha or Arjun.

(c) *Animal and Bird Packs:* Another Ganjifa variety substitutes suitmarks of birds or animals, while retaining the Mir and Vizier court-cards. Some of these animal and bird packs consist of the usual 96 cards, but there are others with a total of 144, containing 12 suits of 12 cards each.

5 *Military Games*

Examples exist of cards from an early military game on the lines of that apparently known to the Emperor Akbar in the sixteenth century. So far as can be judged, the pack was made up of 144 cards divided into 12 suits of 12 cards each. There were 2 court-cards, which, for convenience, we shall call here Mir and Vizier, since these were the titles of the 2 court-cards in Akbar's later 8-suited pack. Suits were divided into two groups, weak and strong. The subjects of the first 8 suits were based on various departments of the imperial court, while the last 4 represented different forms of the deity Shiva.

The 6 strong suits were: *Ashvapati*, Lord of Horses (the Horses suit); *Gajpati*, Lord of Elephants (the Elephants suit); *Narpati*, Lord of Men (the Foot-soldier suit); *Gadhpati*, Lord of Fortresses (the Fortress suit); *Dhanpati*, Lord of Treasures (the Jars of Coins suit); and *Dalpati*, the Lord of Hosts (the Warriors suit).

The 6 weak suits were: *Nawapati*, Lord of Ships (the Ships suit); *Tipati*, Queen with her maids (the Women suit); *Surapati*, Lord of Divinities (the Deities suit); *Asurapati*, Lord of Demons (the Demons suit); *Banpati*, Lord of Beasts (the Animals suit); and *Ahipati*, Lord of Serpents (the Snakes suit).

PLATE 22
Advertising and publicity packs: A. 'Schöner Wohnen' (Better Living) pack by ASS for a German magazine; B. Philips electrical pack, made in Belgium; C. 'Knoll International' geometrical pack from France; D and E. Two Belgian packs with inserts showing deaf-and-dumb alphabets; F. 'Blood Donor' pack by Brépols; G. Sanders 'animal heads' pack by Grimaud; H. 'Boerenbond Veevoeders' farmers' pack by Brépols; J. East German furniture industry pack by VEB Altenburg.

A

B

C

D

E

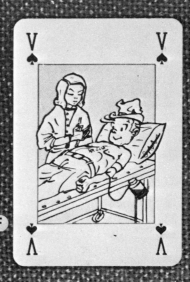

F

G

H

J

79. Indian cards: Ganjifa type from Orissa: Mir and Vizier of Moons suit

6 European-derived Packs

Portuguese, and later, French and British settlement in India led to the introduction of European playing-cards, and certain Indian packs, evidently influenced by the cards used in such games as Hombre and Piquet, came into use. Portuguese-derived packs contain 3 court-cards, King, Knight and Jack (*Rei*, *Cavalo* and *Sota*). Aces, which originally showed the Portuguese Dragon, were retained, but the dragon was transformed into the Indian *Makara*, or croco-dile. Portuguese suitmarks were carried over on to the Indian packs which contain numerical cards 7–2. Cards are rectangular, and about 55mm × 40mm in size.

French-derived packs for playing piquet and bézique were also made, as can be noted from Chad pack No 13. Some of these packs contained an Ace incorporating both the King and Queen, known as *Mariage*. British rule also influenced Indian playing-cards, and some very crude locally made English-type packs were produced.

PERSIAN CARDS

Persian cards are rectangular, and about 50mm × 32mm in size. The traditional Persian pack is called *As Nas*, and is, like Indian cards, hand-painted and lacquered upon materials such as ivory, wood or card. Packs contain 25 cards divided into 5 exactly similar suits:

The *Shah*, or King, appears on a green back-ground; the *Bibi*, or Queen, on a yellow back-ground; the *Couli*, or Dancing Girl, on a red background; the *As* (a lion, eagle or dragon), on a black background, and the *Sarbas*, or Soldier, on a gold background. Other packs exist in which the 5 cards show the same subject, such as a vase of flowers repeated throughout the suit, but with five background colours as shown above.

Ganjifa packs, similar to those used in India, are also known, but they are rectangular, and in the usual Persian size.

80. Persian cards: Couli and Sarbas

11
JAPAN, CHINA AND KOREA

JAPANESE PLAYING-CARDS

Modern Japan produces large numbers of western-type packs of cards both for home use and for export, but there are a number of packs which are peculiarly Japanese, and used only in that country. The arrival of the Portuguese in Japan in the middle of the sixteenth century introduced the first European playing-cards, which were quickly accepted by Japanese players.

Card games, or at least, the idea behind card games, were not unknown to the Japanese, who had from ancient times used painted seashells for similar purposes. The Portuguese packs, having been adopted by the Japanese, gradually became transformed into something typically Japanese.

These Japanese packs, which are still in use today, are much smaller than the European packs from which they were derived, and are printed on very thick card. Similarly, the indigenous Japanese cards too, originally painted on shells, were adapted, and printed on to the same kind of card. These latter packs, called *Hanafuda*, or *Hana Garuta*, are probably the most popular type used in Japan today.

Hana Cards

Packs contain 48 cards measuring about 54mm × 33mm printed on card about 1mm thick. Most packs contain one extra blank card, but a complete set, used by Hana players, consists of two packs, one black-backed, and one red or brown-backed.

Each Hana card bears a different design representing some kind of flower, the pack being divided into 12 suits; one for each month of the year. In addition, certain cards in each suit have additional features, such as birds, animals or other objects, which alter the value of the card. One of these features is the *Tanzaku*, an oblong piece of paper used for writing poetry. Values of the cards are assessed in points; one point being the basic value for cards without special features, others varying between five and twenty points:

Month and Suit	Cards with Special Features		Value in Points
January – Pine	Two:	Crane (bird)	20
		Tanzaku	5
February – Plum	Two:	Nightingale	10
		Tanzaku	5
March – Cherry	Two:	Curtain	20
		Tanzaku	5
April – Wisteria	Two:	Cuckoo	10
		Tanzaku	5
May – Iris	Two:	Bridge	10
		Tanzaku	5
June – Peony	Two:	Butterfly	10
		Tanzaku	5
July – Clover	Two:	Wild Boar	10
		Tanzaku	5
August – Pampas-grass	Two:	Full Moon	20
		Geese	10

September – Chrysanthemum	Two: Wine Cup	10
	Tanzaku	5
October – Maple	Two: Deer	10
	Tanzaku	5
November – Willow or Rain	Four: Poet	20
	Swallow	10
	Tanzaku	5
	Lightning*	1
December – Paulownia	One: Phoenix	20

* This card is also used as a 'wild' or joker, card, with special powers.

81. Hana cards: Cherry Tanzaku and Clover Wild Boar

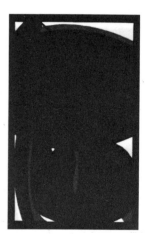

82. Daini pack, featuring the Coin suit

The number of participating players in a Hana game is normally three, but may be as many as six.

Other Japanese packs include varieties of 'matching' games, alphabetical games and those which incorporate classic poems or quotations. Examples of these are:

Hyakunin Isshu, or the 'hundred Poets' game, which contains 100 pairs of cards, making a total of 200 in a pack. Each card shows a Japanese poet or scene, together with an inscription.

Ise Monogatari, or Stories of the *Ise*, a very large pack containing over 400 cards of short classical poems.

E-Awase, or picture-matching cards, with varying numbers of cards to a pack.

Iroha, or alphabet cards, in which 96 cards, half with pictures, half with text, have to be matched together.

European-derived packs

With the passage of 350 years, the original packs of

cards introduced by the Portuguese have become so changed by the Japanese that they are not at first sight comparable with European cards at all. However, close examination reveals their connection, and the suits are distinguishable as Cups (*Koppu*), Swords (*Isu*), Coins (*Oru*), and Batons (*Ho*).

Unsun packs

This pack of 75 cards has very clear suitmarks. There are 5 suits: the normal Cups, Swords, Coins and Batons, and a *Tomoe*, or 'whirligig' suit. In addition to the 3 usual court-cards (King, or *Koshi*, Knight,

A

B

C

D

E

F

G

H

J

or *Uma*, and Jack, or *Sota*), there is a fourth: the Dragon, or *Rohai*; a fifth: the *Un* (god of good fortune), and a sixth: the *Sun* (dignitary). Each suit has numerical cards from 9 to 1 which, with the 6 courts, makes 15. The cards measure about 75mm × 48mm.

Kabu Cards

These packs contain one basic suit repeated four times, normally with one extra, or *shingo*, card. There are 1 to 3 court-cards, with 9 numerical cards, including the Ace, making a pack of either 40 or 48 cards:

Kabu Fuda: This features the Batons (*Ho*) suit. One court-card, and numerical cards 9–2 with the Ace are repeated four times. One of the suits has special overprints on the Four, and sometimes on the Ace and Three. In addition, there is a Demon or *shingo* card, which, together with a blank extra card, makes a total of 42 to the pack.

Daini: This pack features the Coins (*Oru*) suit, and is constituted similarly to the pack above, repeating the suit four times, together with the Demon and blank card. Packs are known with the suit repeated five times.

Komaru: This again features the Coins suit, but instead of repeating the suit four times, the fourth suit contains a Four of Batons (*Ho*), and with an Ace showing a dragon. Basic packs contain 40 cards.

Kudosan: The Coins suit, with 3 court-cards is repeated three times, the fourth suit containing overprinted cards, including a Four of Batons. There is a Demon card, and an extra blank, making 50 cards in all.

Mefuda: This is another variety of the 40-card pack featuring the Coins suit.

Irinokichi: The Batons suit, with 3 court-cards, is repeated three times, while the fourth suit includes a differently designed Ace, and 4 cards overprinted in silver. A Demon card brings the total in a pack up to 49.

PLATE 24
A. 'The Man from UNCLE' pack by Ed-U-Cards, USA; B. General de Gaulle pack by Dorchy, from cartoons by Siné; C. 'The President's Deck' by US Playing Card Co for Alfabet; D, E and F. Circular packs from Japan, United Kingdom and Belgium; G. The 'Jesus' Deck by Müller for Game Masters Inc; H. 'Le Burling' pack by A. Girard, Albigny; J. Cucu pack by Masenghini.

83. Kudosan pack, featuring the Coins suit in a different style

84. Irinokichi pack: featuring the Batons suit

85. Kinseizan pack: Knight and Three of Batons

Kinseizan: Again, this features the Batons suit with 3 court-cards. The suit is repeated three times, with Japanese numerals shown on all but 3 cards. On the fourth suit, silver overprints appear on the 3 court-cards, on the Two and Ace. With the Demon and a blank extra card, the pack totals 50.

Mekuri Cards

Mekuri packs are similar in appearance to Kabu cards, but contain 4 different suits of 12 cards each. Packs currently available are:

Akahachi: This pack contains the 4 suits of Cups (*Koppu*), Swords (*Isu*), Coins (*Oru*), and Batons (*Ho*), with numerical cards 9–2 and Ace in each suit, together with 3 court-cards. The Two of Swords shows the figure of Buddha, while all but the Two and Three bear Japanese numerals. Silver overprints appear on the Eight of Swords, the Two, Three,

Four, Five and Six of Batons and Money, while extra cards include the Demon (*shingo*) and a blank, making a total pack of 50 cards.

Fukutoku: Also containing 4 suits, this has a Baton suit showing silver overprints on all cards. Numerical cards from Four to Nine of the Swords suit show Japanese numerals, while the Two shows a human face towards the top. Silver lines are overprinted on the Two, Three, Four, Five and Ace. The last 4 numerical cards of the Batons suit also show Japanese numerals, and there is an additional Demon card.

Other Mekuri packs are *Komatsu*, which is similar in style to *Akahachi*, *Kurofuda*, similar to *Fukutoku*, *Kurouma*, *Kinyoku* and *Mitsuohgi*.

Kabu and Mekuri cards are usually printed in red, black, silver and sometimes dark blue, with plain backs in black or red.

86. Akahachi pack: King of Cups and Two of Swords   87. Fukutoku pack: Knight, and Four of Cups

CHINESE PLAYING-CARDS

There appears to be no word in the Chinese language for 'playing-cards', which are lumped together with other gaming devices such as dice, dominoes, chess-pieces etc, under a generic title meaning 'objects for gambling'. This sums up the Chinese attitude to playing-cards as just another form of gambling. Chinese cards are thought to have existed at least as early as the T'ang Dynasty (AD 618–907), although we have no real proof of this. They remain very popular with Chinese people in all parts of the

world, except in the People's Republic, where they are regarded with some disfavour, no doubt because of their use in gambling.

The cards are always long and narrow, varying in size from about 65mm × 20mm to something like 120mm × 30mm. They can be classified into six main groups: Mah Jongg cards, Word or Phrase cards, Number cards, Money cards, Domino or Dice cards, and Chess cards.

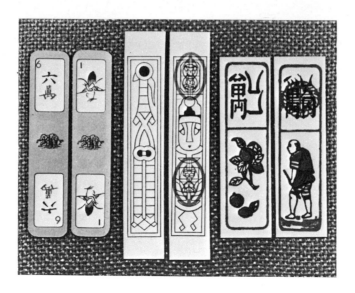

88. Mah Jongg: Six of Characters; and Spring; Tung Kwan Pai: 3 strings of Coins; and 'Joker'; B'at: Money pack from Vietnam

Mah Jongg Cards

These are nothing more than playing-card versions of Mah Jongg tiles, but are much cheaper to buy. The game of Mah Jongg is based on an elaborated version of the three-suited Chinese Money pack. There are 136 cards to a pack, made up of 3 suits of 9 cards repeated four times. In addition, there are 4 Winds and 3 Dragons, also repeated four times.

The 3 suits in Mah Jongg are Bamboos, Circles and Characters, which are numbered from 1 to 9 in Chinese, and sometimes in Arabic numerals as well. The 4 Winds are East, South, West and North, while the Dragons are Red, Green and White. One or two sets of Flower cards are sometimes added, 4 being known as Spring, Summer, Autumn and Winter, and the second 4 being the Fisher, the Woodcutter, the Farmer and the Scholar. With additional cards, a complete Mah Jongg pack can contain 144 cards.

Word, Phrase and Number Cards

These cards are difficult to appreciate without a knowledge of Chinese. The two groups are similar in character, the purpose of the game being to acquire as many cards as possible bearing the same phrase, word or number. Packs are arranged in categories rather than suits, and may consist of upwards of 30 cards, often repeated several times.

Money Cards

Chinese packs based on money usually contain 120 cards, consisting of a basic pack of 30 or 40 cards repeated three or four times. Each of these basic packs have either 3 or 4 suits of 9 cards, together with 3 or 4 'court'-cards in each suit. These suits are related to Chinese coins called *cash*; in fact it is thought that the origin of Chinese playing-cards of this type was an early type of paper money used for gambling.

The suits are: single Coins, Strings of Coins, Myriads of Coins, and variations of these. The Chinese *cash* was a coin made with a hole in the middle, and these coins could be tied with string to make a *tael* (1,000), a myriad (10,000) etc. One myriad was therefore equivalent to ten *tael*. Some examples of Money packs are:

Tung Kwan Pai: A pack from Hong Kong containing 120 cards plus 2 extra cards or jokers. Suits are: Coins, Myriads of Coins, and Thousands of Myriads of Coins. Size 100mm × 19mm.

Ba't: A pack of 38 cards from Vietnam, containing 4 suits of Coins, Hundreds of Coins, Thousands of Coins, and Myriads of Coins. There are 2 extra 'court'-cards. Size 83mm × 24mm.

To Tom: A pack of 120 cards from Vietnam, consisting of 3 suits (Coins, Hundreds of Coins, and Myriads of Coins) repeated four times. Size 100mm × 25mm.

89. Chi Chi Pai: Nine Myriads and Five Myriads: To Tom: Money pack from Vietnam; Hakka Ti Pai: Two myriads and 'Clouded Money' (one coin)

Chi Chi Pai: A pack of 60 cards from Thailand, consisting of two sets of 30. The suits are as for *Tung Kwan Pai*. Size 58mm × 20mm.

Hakka Ti Pai: This is one of several Chinese names given to this pack, an English equivalent being 'Six-Tiger' cards. Packs contain 38 cards made up of 4 suits (Coins, Tens of Coins, Hundreds of Coins, and Thousands of Coins) plus 2 extra cards called *Pai Tzu* (one hundred sons) and *Mao Kung*. The cards, about 20mm × 65mm, are printed in black on white, with some cards bearing a red overprint.

Domino Cards

Domino, or Dice cards, called *Tien Chiu Pai* in Chinese, follow the usual Chinese style, being long and narrow, and about 80mm × 20mm in size, They can be quite plain, or with illustrations in the centre. The principal feature is the 'spot' marking similar to ordinary dominoes. Unlike that game, however, the Chinese use 'spots' in two colours in various combinations, usually black and red. There are 21 basic cards showing different spot combinations, and these are repeated four to six times, so that complete packs will contain 84 or 126 cards, sometimes with one or two added 'joker' or title cards.

Chess Cards

These are based on Chinese chess, which can be either four-sided or two-sided. Cards relating to four-sided chess are called *Soo Sik Pai*, or 'four-suited cards'. They are very plain in appearance showing only the Chinese character denoting each piece which is repeated at each end of the card. Packs contain 28 basic cards, which, as with other Chinese packs, are repeated a number of times. Suits are shown by four colours, the characters being printed in black on tinted card: red, yellow, green and white, with each suit containing 7 cards representing the pieces.

Green and White suits contain the following pieces: *Chiang* (General); *Shih* (Official); *Hsian* (Elephant); *P'ao* (Cannon); *Ma* (Horse); *Chü* (Cart); and *Ping* (Soldier).

Red and Yellow suits are: *Shuai* (General); *Shih* (Official); *Hsiang* (Minister); *P'ao* (Cannon); *Ma* (Horse); *Chü* (Battlewagon); and *Tsu* (Soldier).

Two-sided chess cards are called *Hung Pai* (or 'red' cards). Despite their name, cards are printed in

PLATE 25

Reprint packs: A. Morden's pack of 1676; B. Lenthall's Fortune-telling pack of 1714; C. Marlborough's Victories pack of 1707; D. South Sea Bubble pack of 1720. Packs A–D by Harry Margary, Kent. E. Glorious Revolution pack of 1688; F. Popish Plot pack of 1678. Packs E and F by Cornmarket Press. G. Pasquin's Windkaart pack of 1720; H and J. Two packs originally made in Nuremberg in 1813 by J. E. Backofen.

A — IX — ♥ 9 — Kent.

Length — 60.
Breadth — 30.
Circumference — 170.
Canterb. { D: from Lon — 44. 56.
{ Lattitude — 51. 17.
Facsimile

B — XIII · Nimrod ♦

As 9.
Whether ye absent
be alive
Ment. 17
whether in health
or sick
Gi 12
Whether they shall
return
Di 14
Whether safe and
Free
Tro 19
Whether they shall have
a prosperous Voyage
Facsimile

C — KING ♣

Charles III. King of Spain
born October 1st 1685.
Facsimile

D —

A Lady Pawns her Jewels by her Maid,
And in declining Stock, presumes to Trade,
Till in South Sea at length she Drowns her Gin
And now in Bristol Stones, is glad to shine.
Facsimile

E — ♣ Knave

Reddin standing in ye
Pillory.

F — ♠ III

Whiping Heresy Out
of Windsor Chaple.

G — Knegt ♠

Prins Fredriks
mars, naar Vianen
Ik sla prins Fredriks mars, om met
Als wind soldaten, naar Vianen te
te trekken.

H — ♠ King ♠

J — in Nürnberg

90. Tien Chiu Pai: Domino cards; Soo Sik Pai: Battle-wagon and Soldier; Hung Pai: White General and Red Soldier; Hung Pai: Black Official and White Soldier

(*right*)
91. Korean cards: Three 'General' court-cards from the Crow, Rabbit and Fish suits

various combinations of red, black, white and other colours. There are 2 suits representing the opposing sides, making 14 basic cards. These are usually repeated several times, to make packs which can contain as many as 112 cards.

The pieces on each side are similar to those used in the four-sided game: White: General, Official, Elephant, Cannon, Horse, Battlewagon and Soldier. Black or Red pieces are: General, Official, Minister, Cannon, Horse and Battlewagon.

KOREAN CARDS

Korean playing-cards are somewhat similar in appearance to Chinese, but are very long and narrow, averaging 15mm × 160mm. The cards are printed on card or oiled paper, usually orange in colour and very simple in design. One side of the card is inscribed in black with Korean characters describing the suits, and the other side is either blank or bears a black design depicting a feather or arrow-head. A full pack contains 80 cards, divided into 8 suits of 10, which represent Men, Fish, Crows, Pheasants, Antelopes, Stars, Rabbits and Horses.

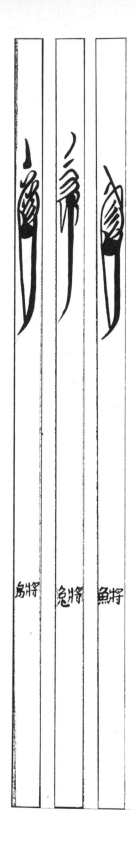

12
NON-STANDARD AND MODERN PLAYING-CARDS

The term 'standard', as used in this book to describe playing-cards, is taken to mean those packs obtainable in any country and used by players of that country in the normal way for card-games. The packs will contain court-cards of a traditional, accepted, pattern, employ the national or international suitmarks, and be of a conventional size. Smaller cards are usually regarded as patience packs.

'Non-standard' is applied to packs which do not conform to the above definition, but which contain cards arranged in definite suits and with recognisable court-cards. In this case, both suitmarks and courts can be fanciful or inventive. Other kinds of cards, as used for games such as 'Snap', 'Old Maid', 'Happy Families', 'Black Peter', 'Quartet', and packs for patented games are not included in either definition, and fall outside the scope of this book.

Early card-makers were inventive, and produced a variety of experimental packs with unusual designs and suitmarks. As we have seen, Germany was responsible for many early non-standard packs, some of which have survived, and can be seen in museums or private collections. A Cologne pack dated 1470 was circular, and contained 5 suits of Hares, Columbines, Pinks, Parrots and Roses; and a beautiful pack in the form of a book was made by Jost Ammon of Nuremberg in 1588, using printers' Inking-pads, Books, Goblets and Vases as suitmarks. The Ambraser Hunting Pack, made in the middle of the fifteenth century, was another pack produced in colours, with suitmarks of Herons, Falcons, Dogs and Shuttlecocks.

With the acceptance of standard cards, this type of pack began to disappear, but during the seventeenth and eighteenth centuries, other kinds of non-standard packs made their appearance in most European countries. In England, the puritanical attitude to card-playing led to the production of packs

with an educational appeal on such subjects as mathematics, geography, astronomy and mythology, while one pack was devoted to lessons on cookery and meat-carving. These packs retained the normal suitmarks, and sometimes a small miniature of a playing-card was shown in the corner of the design.

Other English packs were of a satirical nature, lampooning current fads and fancies, or criticising political and commercial skulduggery. One such pack was concerned with the South Sea Bubble of 1720, another with the Popish Plot of 1678, and there were others based on military exploits.

Similar cards were produced in France, such as the *Jeu de Blason*, a heraldic pack made in 1658 by de Brianville, and several series of educational cards designed by Jean Desmarest in 1644 at the suggestion of Cardinal Mazarin, with subjects like those on the English packs described above.

From Germany came packs reminiscent of the earlier card-makers' triumphs, with suits of Parrots, Hares and Flowers. Others were devoted to political and military matters. In Italy, as in most European countries, there were packs of heraldic cards, and later there were educational series, including one illustrating scenes from the Old Testament, with suits of Circles, Hearts, Diamonds and Vases.

Transformation cards which became popular towards the end of the eighteenth century, were those in which the suitmarks were made to form an integral part of a picture. This was first done by hand on individual packs, but later, packs were specially designed and printed this way. Best-known among these are the Almanac packs issued by Johann Friedrich Cotta, a German publisher of Tübingen.

Cotta's Almanac cards, the first of which appeared in 1804, were designed by the Countess Charlotte von Jennison-Walworth, with the French

A

B

Vierländerin.

Altenau-derin.

Gas-fabrik

C

Dr T Schroeter, Jena

Wappen Rudolfs I

D

V. BUCHBLÄTTER.

E

Roi

Philippe de Bourgogne.

F

G

A Tubinge

chez J. G. Cotta, Libraire

H

suitmarks cleverly incorporated into pictures illustrating scenes from Schiller's play *Die Jungfrau von Orleans*, one on each of 52 cards. Other Almanac packs followed for several years afterwards. The idea was soon taken up by other card-makers, and transformation packs were issued in England, Austria, France and the United States.

The English printer, Thomas de la Rue, was granted a patent in 1832 for a system of printing playing-cards in colour, while in Germany in the following year a firm was founded which was to become one of the best-known producers of playing-cards. This firm was set up by Bernhard Dondorf, a specialist lithographer, and the products included such things as prints, greetings cards, and of course, playing-cards.

'Souvenir' packs are a variety of playing-cards which were in great vogue in the United States during the latter half of the nineteenth century. Apart from the presence of suitmarks and indices, they have little real connection with playing-cards proper, since every card in the pack is given over to a picture, usually of some local place of interest.

Playing-cards have long been used for advertising, usually by designing special backs for the cards, but a more recent development is the adaptation of the face of the cards for advertising purposes.

An American drug firm produced a 'medical' pack, in which the courts were represented by doctors, dentists, nurses and laboratory workers, and a similar idea was developed in France, where a pack showed doctors, nurses and medical students as the court figures. Another French pack, made for a firm of sanitary engineers featured engineers, housewives and plumbers, and a similar firm in Germany produced a pack with the court-card figures holding taps and other items of bathroom equipment.

An Austrian wine company produced a pack with the court figures clutching wine-glasses, tankards and bunches of grapes, while in Germany, a brewery had its courts with the Kings holding pewter tankards, saucy barmaids as Queens, and Jacks with large glass mugs of beer. The Hungarian 'Seasons' pattern was also adapted in a similar way by an Austrian brewery.

The Gala publicity pack, produced in Paris, featured not one advertiser, but sixteen, each of the court-cards and Aces being designed to promote a particular firm. A pharmaceutical firm in Holland sponsored a pack to promote their brands of aspirin and other products, suitably illustrated by humorous court-cards.

Very often, the product itself is not given a 'hard sell', so that it is not always obvious that the pack is, in fact, a publicity one. The Neiman Marcus pack, issued by a Texas department store, is one of these, with humorous courts depicting cowboys, Indians and saloon-girls. A Japanese pack made for a firm making children's dolls shows humorous courts, but only the Jokers really tell us about the product.

A pack produced for a Hamburg shipping firm has various sea-gods, such as Neptune, for Kings, with local beauties for Queens and German sailors as Jacks. Another pack in a similar vein was made for a Dutch maker of marine paint, in which the Kings are sea-captains, the Queens either 'naughty' or formidable ladies, and the Jacks tough members of the crew. Drawings of ships from different countries appear on the Aces.

East Germany has also produced several publicity packs, including one for a newspaper designed by its own cartoonist, Erich Schmitt, while a similar pack in which all 54 cards (with jokers) bear colour cartoons is sponsored by the same newspaper group. Another East German pack was produced for a local furniture factory.

A pack from the United States which aims to publicise drug abuse, devotes all numerical cards to information on the ill-effects of drugs, together with semi-humorous courts with appropriate captions.

The Michelin tyre firm produced a pack in which the courts were all versions of their 'tyre man', and a Japanese heavy industrial concern produced a cartoon-style pack in which the courts featured various pieces of equipment.

Also printed in Japan, and sponsored by the Coca-Cola company, was a special pack to commemorate the various international Scout Jamborees from

PLATE 26
Reprint packs: A. Fifteenth-century Ambraser Hunting pack by Edition Leipzig; B and C. Hamburger Kartenspiel of 1870 by Broschek Verlag, Hamburg; D. Dr Schroeter's nineteenth-century pack with non-standard suitmarks; E. German mining pack, originally made in 1840 by Industrie Comptoir, now issued by the Saxon Mining Museum; F, G and H. Cotta Almanac pack of 1805 by Edition Leipzig.

QUEEN OF COINS

THE LOVERS

QUEEN OF PENTACLES

QUEEN OF COINS

THE LOVERS

LOVERS

LE BATELEUR

LES AMOUREUX &c.3

LE CHARIOR

LE FOL.

1937 to date. One or two packs originating in Belgium and Holland have been produced for farmers' co-operatives and meat-packing firms. In these, the courts have been given comic animals' heads. Horses' heads appear on Hearts, chickens' heads on Clubs, pigs' heads on Diamonds, and cattle heads on Spades. Another pack makes its Kings pigs, its Queens cows, and its Jacks chickens.

Political affairs provide material for both laudatory and lampooning packs of cards. These date from the eighteenth century and even earlier, but one such pack issued in Western Germany had to be withdrawn because of complaints about its content. Another mildly satirical pack was very popular in the United States; it featured the Kennedy family at the time when John F. Kennedy was President.

Another American pack used all 52 cards to portray, in caricature, various domestic politicians and their associates. Among people shown were Presidents Nixon and Johnson, Governor Wallace, Jane Fonda, Bob Hope, Spiro Agnew, Henry Kissinger, Senator Ford and Ronald Regan. A similar pack, known as the 'President's Deck', featured President Nixon, Mrs Nixon and Spiro Agnew, with George Wallace and Hubert Humphrey as jokers.

France produced a pack along the same lines featuring General de Gaulle. Straight humour has been the subject of many packs, some of which are simply a series of cartoons with joke captions. An attractive humorous pack, showing the courts in historical costume, is currently made by the Swedish firm of J. Öberg, and a pleasantly-amusing pack called 'Happy Playing Cards' is made by F. X. Schmid of Munich.

A humorous adaptation of the Spanish pack comes from a firm in Madrid, which features cartoon-like courts depicting Don Quixote and Sancho Panza, together with vignettes on the numerical cards. Walt Disney characters appear on a number of packs, including one from Italy, in which Mickey Mouse, Donald Duck, Goofy and others figure on the courts.

The cartoonist Mingote has designed two comic packs for the Spanish firm of Myr, one pack with French suits, and an entirely different one with Spanish suitmarks. In Germany, ASS has issued a Skat pack with 'wicked' comedy courts designed by the cartoonist Loriot.

A strange-looking, but humorous pack, whose courts have faces made up of odds and ends of bones, eyes, numbers, ships and birds, was designed by Salvador Dali for a French firm, while another odd-looking design, identified by the name Nespolo, appeared in Italy. Surrealist faces are accompanied by adaptations of the French suitmarks, in which the Clubs have been transformed into purple rosettes.

From Japan has come a 'Western' pack, with cartoon-style representations of well-known characters like Wild Bill Hickok, Wyatt Earp, Buffalo Bill, Jesse James, Calamity Jane and Annie Oakley on the court cards.

Historical themes lend themselves admirably to playing-card design, and a recent pack, with court-cards based on late eighteenth-century political cartoons, was made by a Belgian firm for the Royal Pavilion, Brighton. A large French production, consisting of two packs issued together under the title *Jeu de Blocus*, features personalities of the Napoleonic Wars. Court-cards depict Francis II, Emperor of Austria (Holy Roman Empire), the Archduke Charles, Admiral Nelson, the Duke of Wellington, and Lady Hamilton, while numerical cards have colour pictures of soldiers from the armies of Austria-Hungary, Prussia, England, Scotland, Russia and France. The Jokers are Napoleon and the Tsar of Russia.

The Napoleonic theme has been used in a number of packs, among them one issued in 1969 by Grimaud of Paris to celebrate the 200th birthday of the Emperor. Napoleon appears as the King of Hearts, and Josephine as the Queen. Other Kings are close associates or members of the Buonaparte family; Jerome of Westphalia, Murat-Napoleon, King of Naples, and Louis, King of Holland, while their consorts appear as Queens, with various Dukes and Princes as Jacks. The Aces show orders and decorations of the Empire.

In 1962 the firm of Catel & Farcy issued another Napoleonic pack, this one showing Buonaparte as the King of Clubs, and the rest of the courts with members of the family or royal court. Yet another

A

B

THE LOVERS

C

THE LOVERS.

D

QUEEN of PENTACLES

QUEEN OF PENTACLES

E

F

G

Homme blond, aimable.
Pour une consultante : mari,
fiancé ou ami. Pour un consul-
tant : ami, protecteur).

Près de
♥ : il est aimant, fidèle, confiant
heureux. DAME ♥ : songe au
mariage ou à donner preuve
d'amour.
♣ : généreux, aide dans vie
matérielle.
DAME ♦ : Intrigues sans influence sur lui. -
AUTRE ♦ : Protecteur influent ou supérieur
bienveillant Grand appui dans situation.
♠ : aide, conseille utilement pour soucis graves.

H

FURTO

J

pack was issued in 1971 in Italy, containing 40 cards of a long, narrow type, on which the courts show Napoleon as the King of Hearts and Josephine as the Queen. The rest portray members of the army or court, and each suitmark incorporates the initial 'N'.

A very attractive double pack with an historical basis was issued in 1970 by John Waddington of Leeds. A limited edition, this was produced to commemorate the 200th anniversary (in 1976) of the crossing of the Delaware in the American War of Independence. Called 'Grand Slam', one pack features prominent American leaders of the time, and the other has leaders from the British side. Among those appearing are four Presidents: George Washington, John Adams, James Madison and Thomas Jefferson; and Lord North, the Earl of Sandwich, Earl Cornwallis and King George III.

Piatnik of Vienna produced an interesting pack in 1953 which shows a number of figures from European history. The court figures are represented by Marie Antoinette, Madame Pompadour, Louis XIV of France, Duke of Marlborough, the Empress Maria Theresa, Frederick the Great and others. A similar pack is called 'Tudor Rose', issued to commemorate the coronation of Queen Elizabeth II. This has various figures from English history on the courts, including Henry VIII and Anne Boleyn, Queen Anne, Sir Francis Drake, Elizabeth I, Disraeli, Edward VII and Queen Victoria.

French history is featured on the 'Versailles' pack, whose courts have Kings or Queens associated with the famous palace, the Jacks honouring the architects who designed it. Similarly, the pack entitled 'Val de Loire' shows historical personalities associated with the Loire country during the Renaissance, including England's Henry VIII, Catherine de Medici, and Henry II of France. Aces show famous chateaux of the area.

From Belgium in 1934 came a pack showing four generations of the Belgian royal family, the most recent personalities appearing on the Hearts suit,

which has Leopold as King, and Astrid as Queen. On the Spades suit, the King and Queen are Albert I and Elizabeth, while the Jacks are royal servants.

A pack featuring operas by Wagner was prepared in 1920 but never issued, but in 1968, a Swiss playing-card collector, Dr Brum-Antonioli, commissioned a special print of the pack in a limited edition. The same collector also sponsored the 'Alchemist' pack in 1967 in which the courts featured Kings and Knaves performing various tasks connected with alchemy. Vignetted drawings also appear on the Aces and numerical cards. Both packs were made in Switzerland.

From that country, too, comes an attractive costume pack, on which the courts have figures wearing the dress of a particular canton, together with pictorial Aces, each showing two Swiss views. A comparable Austrian pack shows people wearing provincial costumes, while a pack from Iceland shows leading personalities from the country's early history. This pack also has pictorial Aces showing Icelandic scenes. A pack called 'Bretagne', issued by Grimaud of Paris, shows folk costumes from that province.

Sporting subjects have not been neglected by card-makers. A 'sharpshooters' pack was produced in Germany in 1966 to celebrate a small-arms shooting championship, with the designs showing marksmen and targets, while a Japanese pack uses all the cards to illustrate fifty-two sports and athletic activities. At least one pack is based on association football. Made in Germany, this has players and female supporters as courts, and shows alternative French and non-standard suits of Cups, Footballs, Pennants and Trophies. A French pack, issued to publicise a sports firm, has suits of Rugby balls (Hearts); Soccer balls (Clubs); Satchels (Diamonds); and Tennis Shoes (Spades).

Even religion has found its way on to packs of cards. In 1950, two packs were issued in Australia, in which each card contained a picture of a religious event, together with appropriate text, from the Bible. One pack deals with the Old Testament, and one with the New. Normal indices and suitmarks are shown on each card.

In 1973, a new religious pack appeared in the United States, in which the normal suitmarks are replaced by a symbol appropriate to one of the four Evangelists, Matthew, Mark, Luke and John. Called

PLATE 28
Tarot and fortune-telling packs: A and B. 'Egyptian' tarot by the Church of Light, Los Angeles; C and F. Tarot 'Classic' by Müller; D and E. The Waite Tarot, designed by Pamela Colman Smith; G. 'Oracle' fortune-telling pack by Héron; H. 'Lenormand' pack by ASS; J. 'Il Vostro Destino' pack by Viassone.

the 'Jesus' deck, the pack contains 54 cards, each one of which illustrates an event from the New Testament.

Although some of the early non-standard packs are out of reach of most collectors, it is now possible to obtain good reprints of many. A beautiful version, printed in seven colours, has been made in East Germany of the sixteenth-century Jost Ammon pack. The reproduced pack has been made from an original one in a Dresden museum, except for 2 cards out of the 52 which are missing, but which are included in the new pack in black and white. The same firm also reproduced the Ambraser Hunting pack of fifteenth-century Germany, the pack containing 54 of the original 56 cards.

Other German reproductions include the Cotta Almanac transformation pack of 1805, and the Hamburger Kartenspiel, another transformation pack dating from 1870. More recently, there have been cheaper reprints of the nineteenth-century Schroeter and Backofen packs. Recently, too, a Belgian firm issued a reproduction of the Mameluke pack from the Topkapi Sarayi museum in Istanbul, together with extra reconstructed cards not found in the original pack.

The 1906 Ditha Moser tarot pack has been reprinted in Vienna, and a pack of Spanish-suited playing-cards, originally drawn on leather by Apache Indians, was reproduced by Harold and Virginia Wayland of Pasadena, California, who were also responsible for reprints of the seventeenth-century English 'Meal Tub Plot' and Winstanley geographical packs.

From Edizione del Solleone, operated by the Italian collector and printer Vito Arienti, have appeared reprints of an eighteenth-century *tarocchino* pack, together with *Pasquins Windkaart*, originally made in Holland in 1720, and several other rare and early packs from Italy and France.

In England, Harry Margary has reprinted Morden's geographical pack of 1676, Marlborough's Victories pack of 1707, the South Sea Bubble cards of 1720, and John Lenthall's Fortune-Telling pack of 1712. Cornmarket Press also published in England the *Compleat Gamester*, a reprint of a book by Charles Cotton, which originally appeared in 1674. Included with the book are two reprint packs of cards, the Popish Plot pack of 1678, and the Glorious Revolution pack of 1688.

PLATE 29
The Worshipful Company of Makers of Playing Cards in London issues an annual pack with a special commemorative back design, and with the portrait of the Master on the Ace of Spades. This is a selection of some back designs.

ADDENDA

Recent research and study of the history of playing-cards has meant that some additions and modifications are needed to the text in the preceding pages. The author is indebted to members of the Playing-Card Society for this information.

Latin suit-systems

At the Rye Convention of the Playing-Card Society in 1973, it was agreed that the suitmarks of Cups, Swords, Coins and Batons should be given a generic title of 'Latin', but that this should be sub-divided into: Latin/Italian, Latin/Italo-Spanish, Latin/Italo-Portuguese and Latin/Archaic.

The first two sub-divisions apply to the systems described in this book as 'Italian suitmarks' and 'Italo-Spanish suitmarks'. Some explanation is needed for the second two:

Italo-Portuguese: The suitmarks are mainly identified as having straight Swords in that suit, similar to Italo-Spanish, but with the Swords crossed. In two or all of the suits in some packs the Jack is replaced by a Maid. Packs falling into this category include some early Italian Tarot and Trappola packs, Florentine Minchiate packs, obsolete Portuguese packs (with offspring in Brazil and Japan) and the existing Sicilian Tarot pack.

Archaic: This type is known on a few fifteenth-century sheets of Italian cards. The suitmarks for Swords (which are curved) touch each other, but do not cross. Compare the Swords on the Mameluke pack.

German-suited packs

Several other German-suited packs have been noted, including the Oedenburg/Sopron, the Tiroler, and the Lemberger, but descriptions were not available to the writer when this book went to press.

French-suited Tarots

A third type of Austrian standard Tarot (*Industrie und Glück*) has been identified. The variations may be noted by referring to Tarot No III, which reveals:

Style A: Soldier with corn sheaf
Style B: Gondola scene
Style C: Well scene

Style A has been made in Austria, Czechoslovakia, and Germany, Style B in Austria and Hungary, and Style C in Austria, Hungary and Poland.

APPENDICES

1 MUSEUMS AND SOCIETIES

Museums

Austria: Albertina Library, Vienna
Kunsthistorisches Museum, Vienna
Stadt-Museum, Linz

Belgium: Bibliothèque Royale, Brussels
Musée de la Carte à Jouer, Turnhout

England: The Bodleian Library, Oxford
The British Museum, London
The Castle Museum, Norwich
The Guildhall, London
The Pitt-Rivers Museum, Oxford
Stationers' Hall, London
Victoria and Albert Museum, London

France: Bibliothèque de l'Arsenal, Paris
Bibliothèque de l'Ecole Nationale
Supérieure des Beaux-Arts, Paris
Bibliothèque Municipale, Rouen
Bibliothèque Nationale, Paris
The Louvre, Paris
Musée des Arts Decoratifs, Paris
Musée Carnavalet, Paris

Germany, East: Schlossmuseum, Altenburg

Germany, West: Bayerisches Nationalmuseum, Munich
Deutsches Spielkarten-Museum,
Stuttgart
Germanisches National-Museum,
Nuremberg

Historisches Museum, Frankfurt
Museum für Kunsthandwerk,
Frankfurt

Spain: Museo de Naipes, Vitoria

Switzerland: Historisches Museum, Basle

USA: Beinecke Library, Yale University,
New Haven, Connecticut
Cincinnati Art Museum, Cincinnati,
Ohio
Metropolitan Museum of Art, New
York City
National Gallery of Art, Washington,
DC
National Museum, Washington, DC
Pierpont Morgan Library, New York
City
Smithsonian Institution, Washington,
DC
Yale University Library, New Haven
Connecticut

Societies

Chicago Playing Card Collectors Inc, 1407 South 58th
Avenue, Cicero, Illinois 60650, USA

Gruppo Nazionale Giocofilia dell'Unione Nazionale
Collezionisti d'Italia, Torre dei Conti, Largo Corrado
Ricci 44, 00184 Rome, Italy

The Playing-Card Society, 178 Frankley Beeches Road,
Birmingham B31 5LW, England

2 MANUFACTURERS

The following manufacturers have been referred to in the
book, usually by some brief form of their names, which
are here given in full. Many of these companies are no
longer in existence.

ASS   Vereinigte Altenburger und Stralsunder
Spielkarten-Fabriken AG, Leinfelden-
bei-Stuttgart, West Germany

Bielefeld   Bielefelder Spielkarten GmbH,
Bielefeld, West Germany

Biermans   Usines Biermans SA, Turnhout,
Belgium

Brépols   Usines Brépols SA, Turnhout, Belgium

Cambissa	Cambissa e Cia, Trieste, Italy	Modiano	Modiano Industrie Cartotecniche, SpA, Trieste, Italy
Camoin	A. Camoin & Cie, Marseilles, France	Müller	J. Müller & Cie SA, Schaffhausen, Switzerland
Casino	Casino, Prague, Czechoslovakia	Nintendo	Nintendo Playing Card Co Ltd, Kyoto, Japan
Catel & Farcy	Catel & Farcy, Paris, France	Öberg	J. O. Öberg & Son AB, Eskilstuna, Sweden
Dal Negro	Teodomiro Dal Negro, Treviso, Italy	OTK	Obchodní Tiskárny np, Kolín, Prague, Czechoslovakia
De La Rue	Thomas De La Rue & Co Ltd, London, England	Piatnik	Ferdinand Piatnik & Söhne, Vienna, Austria
Dondorf	B. Dondorf GmbH, Frankfurt, Germany	Plastic Cards	Plastic Cards, Milan, Italy
Edition Leipzig	Deutscher Buch-Export und -Import GmbH, Leipzig, East Germany	Speelkaarten Nederland	Speelkaartenfabriek 'Nederland', Amsterdam, Netherlands
Fournier	Heraclio Fournier SA, Vitoria, Spain	Triboulet	Le Triboulet, Paris, France
F. X. Schmid	F. X. Schmid Vereinigte Spielkarten-fabriken KG, Munich, West Germany	US Playing Card Co	US Playing Card Co, Cincinnati, Ohio, USA
GKM Leningrad	State Playing-card Monopoly, Leningrad, USSR	Van Genechten	nv Van Genechten, Turnhout, Belgium
Goodall	Chas Goodall & Son Ltd, London, England	VEB Altenburg	VEB Altenburger Spielkartenfabrik, Altenburg, East Germany
Grimaud	B. P. Grimaud, Paris, France	Viassone	A. Viassone, Turin, Italy
Héron	Société Boechat, Bordeaux, France	VSS Altenburg	Vereinigte Stralsunder Spielkarten-fabriken, Altenburg, Germany (pre-World War II)
Holmblad	Holmblads Spillekort Forretning, S. Salomon & Co, Copenhagen, Denmark	John Waddington	John Waddington Ltd, Leeds, England
KZWP	Krakowskie Zaktady Wyborów Papierowych, Cracow, Poland		
Masenghini	Ditta Masenghini di Lombardia, Bergamo, Italy		

BIBLIOGRAPHY

Allemagne, Henry-René d'. *Les Cartes à jouer du XIVe au XXe siècle*. Paris: Hachette, 1906

Benham, W. Gurney. *Playing Cards*. London: Ward Lock, 1931

——. *A Short History of Playing Cards*. Published by the author, c 1932

Chatto, William Andrew. *Facts and Speculations on the Origin and History of Playing Cards*. London: John Russell Smith, 1848

Clébert, Jean-Paul. *The Gypsies*. London: Studio Vista, 1964

Court de Gébelin, Antoine. *Le Monde primitif*, Vol III. Paris: 1781

Culin, Stewart. *Chinese Games with Dice and Dominoes*. Washington, DC: Smithsonian Institution, 1895

——. *Korean Games*. Philadelphia, Pa: University of Pennsylvania, 1895

——. *The Game of Ma-jong: Its Origin and Significance*. New York: Brooklyn Museum, 1924

Fournier, Félix Alfaro. *Museo de Naipes*. Victoria: Heraclio Fournier, 1972

Hargrave, Catherine Perry. *A History of Playing Cards*. New York: Houghton Mifflin, 1930; and New York: Dover, 1966

Hase, Martin von. *Spielkarten aus aller Welt*. Stuttgart: Staatsgalerie, 1968

Hoffman, Detlef. *Spielkartensammlung Piatnik*. Vienna: Piatnik, 1970

——. *Spielkarten des Historischen Museums Frankfurt am Main*. Frankfurt: 1972

——. *The Playing Card*. Edition Leipzig, 1973

Hoffman, D., and Kroppenstedt, E. *Französische Spielkarten des XX. Jahrhunderts*. Bielefeld: Deutsches Spielkarten-Museum, 1967

——. *Die Cotta'schen Spielkarten-Almanache 1805–1811*. Bielefeld: Deutsches Spielkarten-Museum, 1969

——. *Inventar-Katalog der Spielkarten-Sammlung des Stadtmuseums Linz*. Bielefeld: Deutsches Spielkarten-Museum, 1969

——. *Wahrsagekarten*. Bielefeld: Deutsches Spielkarten-Museum, 1972

Huson, Paul. *The Devil's Picturebook*. London: Abacus, 1972

Jandin, Cécile de (ed). *Catalogue de la donation Paul Marteau*. Paris: Bibliothèque Nationale, 1966

Janssen, Han. *Speelkaarten*. Bussum: Ć. A. J. van Dishoeck, 1965

Kaplan, Stuart R. *Tarot Cards for Fun and Fortune Telling*. New York: US Games Systems, 1970

Leek, Sybil. *Numerology, the Magic of Numbers*. New York: Collier Books, 1969

Lévi, Eliphas. *Dogme et rituel de la haute magie*. Paris: 1856

Leyden, Rudolf von. *Chad, the Playing Cards of Mysore*. Published by the author, 1973

Mann, Sylvia. *The William Penn Collection of Playing Cards*. Rye: Published by the author, 1966

——. *Collecting Playing Cards*. London: Howard Baker, 1973

——. *The Dragons of Portugal*. Farnham: Sandford, for the Playing-Card Society, 1973

Mayer, L. A. *Mamluk Playing Cards*. Leiden: E. J. Brill, 1971

Merlin, R. *Origine des cartes à jouer*. Paris: Chez l'Auteur, 1869

Morley, H. T. *Old and Curious Playing Cards*. London: Batsford, 1931

O'Donoghue, Freeman M. *Catalogue of the Collection of Playing Cards in the British Museum: Lady Charlotte Schreiber*. London: Longmans, Green, 1901

Omasta, V., and Ravik, S. *Hráči, karty, karetní hry*. Prague: Czech Playing-Card Monopoly(?), 1969

Papus. *The Tarot of the Bohemians*. London: Chapman & Hall, 1892

Pinder, Eberhard. *Charta Lusoria*. Biberach an der Ris: Basoderm, 1961

Prunner, Gernot. *Ostasiatische Spielkarten*. Bielefeld: Deutsches Spielkarten-Museum, 1969

Reisig, Otto. *Deutsche Spielkarten*. Leipzig: Bibliographisches Institut, 1935

Rosenfeld, Helmut. *Munchner Spielkarten um 1500*. Bielefeld: Deutsches Spielkarten-Museum, 1958

Schreiber, Lady Charlotte. *Playing Cards of Various Ages and Countries: Collection of Lady Charlotte Schreiber*. London: John Murray, 1892–5

Seguin, Jean-Pierre. *Le Jeu de carte*. Paris: Hermann, 1968

Singer, Samuel Weller. *Researches into the History of Playing Cards*. London: Robert Triphook, 1816

Taylor, Rev E. S. *The History of Playing Cards*. London: John Camden Hotten, 1865; Rutland, Vt: Chas. E. Tuttle, 1973

Tilley, Roger. *Playing Cards*. London: Weidenfeld & Nicolson, 1967

——. *A History of Playing Cards*. London: Studio Vista, 1973

Toyoshima, Soschichi (ed). *Hanafuda, the Flower Card Game*. Tokyo: Japan Publications, 1970

Trumpf, Peter. *Die Spielkarte*. Stuttgart: VASS, 1957

Van Rensselaer, Mrs John King. *The Devil's Picture Books*. London: T. Fisher Unwin, 1892

Willshire, William Hughes. *A History of Playing and Other Cards in the British Museum*. Edinburgh: Trustees of the BM, 1876

PERIODICALS

Journal of the Playing-Card Society

Bulletin of Chicago Playing Card Collectors, Inc

Le Jolly Joker: 127 rue du Chateau, 92 Boulogne-sur-Seine, France

Playing Cards since 1850: Franz Braun, Klarenbachstrasse 166, 5 Köln-Lindenthal, West Germany

ACKNOWLEDGEMENTS

I would like to express my thanks to: Miss Sylvia Mann for help, advice and the loan of a number of rare playing-cards used for illustrations; Dr Rudolf von Leyden for the use of information contained in his excellent monograph on Chad playing-cards; Mr Ben Zsoldos, of Budapest; Mr Maurice Collett, of Kendal; Herr Kurt Schultze, of the Schlossmuseum, Altenburg; Mr Stuart R. Kaplan, of New York; Mlle Cécile de Jandin, of the Bibliothèque Nationale, Paris; Sr Vito Arienti, Milan; Messrs Ferdinand Piatnik & Sons, of Vienna; F. X. Schmid, of Munich; Catel & Farcy, of Paris; J.-M. Simon of Paris; J. Müller & Cie, of Schaffhausen; Vereinigte Altenburger und Stralsunder Spielkartenfabriken AG, of Stuttgart; Deutscher Buch-Export und -Import GmbH, of Leipzig, and Krakowskie Zaktady Wyrobów Papierowych, of Cracow.

INDEX

Page numbers in *italic* refer to illustrations